NOW FOR THE GOOD NEWS

Robert Dougall's face and voice must be among the best known in Britain. He was on the staff of the BBC from 1933 to 1973, with the exception of four years' service in the Royal Navy during the war, and is remembered as the Senior Television Newsreader, gaining the Top Newscaster Award.

His best-selling autobiography *In and Out of the Box* was published in 1973.

Since retiring from the BBC he has worked as a freelance broadcaster and writer and has appeared regularly as presenter of Yorkshire Television's popular 'Stars on Sunday'.

His interest in birdlife is well known and he served as President of the Royal Society for the Protection of Birds, the largest conservation body in the country, from 1970 to 1975.

NOW FOR THE GOOD NEWS

ROBERT DOUGALL

Collins
FOUNT PAPERBACKS

First published by A. R. Mowbray & Co Limited 1976
First issued by Fount Paperbacks 1978
Second Impression March 1979

© Robert Dougall 1976

Made and printed in Great Britain by
William Collins Sons & Co Ltd, Glasgow

CONTENTS

Introduction   vii
1 THE SPIRIT OF MANKIND   1
2 SOME MANNER OF JOY   37
3 LOVE AND FRIENDSHIP   75
4 COURAGE IN ADVERSITY   107
5 NEW BEGINNINGS   129
Acknowledgements   144
Index   147

INTRODUCTION

It was for me good fortune that my autobiography *In and Out of the Box* was published by the House of Collins. Sir William is sadly with us no more, but I am doubly fortunate in that Lady Collins, his beloved 'Pierre', has given her blessing to this my anthology of inspirational verse and prose which now appears in paperback.

The title is self-explanatory: after twenty years as the nightly messenger on television – bringing more often than not the bad news – it is indeed good news to sing another tune.

During my professional preoccupation with the daily dose of disaster, I think it was only frequent contact with the countryside and the rhythm of natural things that helped me keep life in true perspective. There were times when it would have been easy to despair: it seemed as if the quality of life was being devalued along with the pound. Certainly, in some ways, there has been a marked decline in national morale. And yet, Britain, in spite of largely self-inflicted problems, remains I think one of the most compassionate and caring communities in the world today. Unfortunately, this is an aspect of life that seldom gets reflected in the News.

Although the version of the day's events shown nightly on television gives, of course, the truth and nothing but the truth, it cannot often give the whole truth because of unavoidable editing and timing restrictions. In some ways, it is an image reflected by a distorting mirror; television has an inevitable, built-in bias that operates against the free world. This is simply because the totalitarian states make it their business to maintain a virtual news black-out on all aspects of life not showing them in a good light. In the West, on the other hand, all our negative features are given saturation coverage. It is no wonder if some of our citizens, disenchanted with conditions here, interpret the absence of visible mayhem from authoritarian regimes as confirming their own wishful thinking that somewhere the grass is greener.

In pursuit of a mirage, these often well-intentioned, though deluded, folk somehow contrive to ignore all the firm evidence from that quarter of oppression, hypocrisy, philistinism and jingoistic nationalism. If only they would ask themselves a simple question. Why do the totalitarian states in Eastern Europe and elsewhere find it necessary to bar their subjects from leaving? Why do they hem them in with every conceivable physical restriction—unscalable walls, barbed wire, minefields, sophisticated electronic weaponry, sentries, dogs? Of course, if they didn't, what a mighty rush to freedom there would be!

Even allowing for the fact that it is not easy for any Russian to understand fully the workings of the western mind, it is not to be wondered at that Alexander Solzhenitsyn has expressed dismay at the way we take our ancient freedoms for granted. As he said: 'Once I used to hope that experience of life could be handed on, nation to nation; but now I am beginning to have doubts. Perhaps everyone is fated to live through every experience himself in order to understand.'

As it happens, I know that I myself would never have understood had I not been based up in North Russia for eighteen months or so during war service in the Royal Navy. For all of us there it was a searing experience to see a land gripped by an iron tyranny of fear. Daily, we watched in shocked, impotent silence as the human wrecks from Stalin's Arctic slave camps stumbled, zombie-like, through the snow. Beside them stumped stocky, pink-faced Red Army men— automatic rifles at the ready. There is surely nothing to equal a longish stay in a regimented society of that kind to reinforce a belief in the Western way of life, based on a respect for the individual and owing more than we realise to a Christian background.

How astonishing and wonderful it is that, even after fifty years of state mind-control and terror, men like Solzhenitsyn, Sakharov, Bukhovsky and thousands of other heroes and heroines of the dissident movement have somehow kept deep within themselves a burning knowledge of the difference between good and evil, truth and falsehood. They have shown that, come what may, for some men and women the spirit can never be crushed into a soulless conformity. That is one great cause for hope. Perhaps the inspiration of their steadfast courage and faith will now jolt the West into valuing and cherishing its hard-won freedoms before it is too late. As Wordsworth once reminded us:

'We must be free or die, who speak the tongue
That Shakespeare spake; the faith and morals hold
Which Milton held.'

If life has taught me that individual and religious freedoms are corner-stones for happiness, so too is a belief in the family. Young people need a framework and background for their lives as much as they ever did, perhaps even more so. There is no substitute for the love and security a happy home-life can give.

There will also be reflected here a love of all natural things, especially animals and birds. They have so much to teach us. It seems to me that one of the really hopeful signs in Britain over the pasty twenty years or so has been the upsurge of interest in attempts to conserve the beauty of our countryside and its wildlife. Certainly, the mass concern for birds is comparatively new.

When I first joined the Society for the Protection of Birds in 1950 there were only about 6,000 members. Today, they number over a quarter of a million. Natural history is one of the fields in which radio and television excel, and this is surely an aspect of the broadcasting output that is beyond criticism. It is, moreover, an interest shared by people of all kinds, and most important of all, by the young. During my five-year term as President of the Society, I had many indications of this.

On one occasion it took the form of a telephone call to the BBC news studio at Television Centre. I was busy with the hectic, last-minute preparation before the Nine o'Clock News when I was told there was an urgent call from Northern Ireland. Fearing yet another disaster, I rushed to the telephone to find it was a man from Belfast telling me in anxious tones that his small daughter had that afternoon found a baby starling. What should he do with it? I regret to say that, in the circumstances, I very nearly told him!

And yet, on reflection, perhaps it was he who had got his priorities right. Thousands of ordinary people are turning to nature in reaction to the mindless, impersonal bureaucracy that increasingly governs their lives. Many feel isolated: there is nothing with which they can identify. In some districts the small shops are going; the family doctor has no time for a chat; the parson is shared with another parish, and the old, in particular, are often left with little but an electronic image on television for company. A social worker told me he had recently called on an elderly lady who lived high up in a tower-block. As he opened the door, to his dismay, she promptly burst into tears. Apologetically, she explained that he was the first person she had seen for three weeks.

At last, I believe it is being realised that in housing, education, local government, industry and in fact all organised society big is not necessarily beautiful. There are those, admittedly, who are tempted to think that some monolithic, political panacea will solve all our problems. But it seems to me that the only remedy lies within each individual's power. Instead of trying to set the whole world to rights, it might be more helpful to remember the conclusion Voltaire's Candide came to at the end of his search for the ultimate truth and happiness:

'Il faut cultiver notre jardin.'

If only each one of us did indeed 'cultivate our garden' and attend to our own affairs as well as we knew how, many of the big problems would probably just go away.

For too long, as a nation, we have been living not only on borrowed funds, but also on our reserves of Christian capital. At some time I suppose most people have asked themselves: 'Is there a God?' And usually only a long experience of life with its share of joy and sorrow can help to provide an answer. In my case, I suppose a thorough-going churchman might, if he were charitable, describe me as a devout agnostic. All the same, in spite of reservations about dogma, God remains for me an ever-present yet mysterious being, who pervades all life in the universe and in whom I put my trust. In spite of all the fantastic advances of science, I somehow doubt whether the final answer will ever be found in laboratory experiments. Each individual has to find his or her own way and may feel at the end, as the great Swiss psy-chiatrist Jung did:

> 'I cannot prove it; I just know.'

Personally, I say thank the Lord for a sense of wonder, how-ever child-like it may be.

In this anthology then there is, I trust, a predominantly cheerful tone: the Christian message of hope, a delight in natural things, some flashes of inspiration and, withal, a high degree of serendipity. Horace Walpole coined that word in the eighteenth century and it means 'the faculty of making happy and unexpected discoveries by accident', which is exactly what I hope the reader will be able to do in these pages. So—now for the good news!

SECTION ONE

SECTION ONE

THE SPIRIT OF MANKIND

It is said that for two-thirds of the people of this country the main source of information is television news. So how about beginning with a reminder of some wise words by that many-sided genius William Blake?

> Joy & Woe are woven fine,
> A Clothing for the soule divine.
> Under every grief & pine
> Runs a joy with silken twine.
>
> *William Blake (1757–1827): 'Augeries of Innocence'*

Now, we may like to remember these words from the Epistle of Paul the Apostle to the Philippians:

> Brethren, whatsoever things are true, whatsoever
> things are honest, whatsoever things are just, what-
> soever things are pure, whatsoever things are lovely,
> whatsoever things are of good report; if there be any
> virtue, and if there be any praise, think on these
> things.
>
> *Philippians 4: 8*

There are certain people we meet whose lives seem to be inspired by an inner light. As Louis Pasteur, the great French
research chemist of the last century, put it:

> Blessed is he who carries within himself a God, an
> ideal of beauty, and who obeys it; ideal of art, ideal of
> science, ideal of the fatherland, ideal of the virtues of
> the Gospel, for therein lie the springs of great
> thoughts and great actions; they all reflect light from
> the Infinite.
>
> *Pasteur, in his reception oration at*
> *the Académie des Sciences*

How important it is and how difficult to achieve—the perfect
balance between society and solitude. There are many today
who even find silence intolerable, let alone solitude—hence,
I suppose, the craze for piped music and transistors. And yet,
I would say: 'Be still and listen to the heartbeat of the universe.' Philip Gilbert Hamerton writing in 1873 put it like
this:

> We need society, and we need solitude also, as we
> need summer and winter, day and night, exercise and
> rest. I thank heaven for a thousand pleasant and
> profitable conversations with acquaintances and
> friends; I thank heaven also, and not less gratefully,
> for thousands of sweet hours that have passed in
> solitary thought or labour, under the silent stars.
>   Society is necessary to give us our share and place
> in the collective life of humanity, but solitude is
> necessary to the maintenance of the individual life.
> Society is to the individual what travel and commerce

are to a nation, during which it develops its especial originality and genius.

The life of the perfect hermit, and that of those persons who feel themselves nothing individually, and have no existence but what they receive from others, are alike imperfect lives. The perfect life is like that of a ship of war which has its own place in the fleet and can share in its strength and discipline, but can also go forth alone in the solitude of the infinite sea. We ought to belong to society, to have our place in it, and yet to be capable of a complete individual existence outside of it.

Which of the two is the grander, the ship in the disciplined fleet, arranged in order of battle, or the ship alone in the tempest, a thousand miles from land? The truest grandeur of the ship is in neither one nor the other, but in the capacity for both. What would that captain merit who either had not seamanship enough to work under the eye of the admiral, or else had not sufficient knowledge of navigation to be trusted out of range of signals.

I value society for the abundance of ideas that it brings before us, like carriages in a frequented street; but I value solitude for sincerity and peace, and for the better understanding of the thoughts that are truly ours.

Philip Gilbert Hamerton (1834–1894):
'The Intellectual Life'

Men and women have always been dreamers of dreams—long before the holiday travel bonanza got going over the media. Here is a splendid dream of a paradise island dreamt by an unknown poet lost in the age-old Celtic mists of time.

There is an island far away, around which the sea-horses glisten, flowing on their white course against its shining shore; four pillars support it.

It is a delight to the eye, the plain which the hosts frequent in triumphant ranks; coracle races against chariot in the plain south of Findargad.

Pillars of white bronze are under it, shining through aeons of beauty, a lovely land through the ages of the world, on which many flowers rain down.

Colours of every hue gleam throughout the soft familiar fields; ranged round the music, they are ever joyful in the plain south of Argadnél.

Weeping and treachery are unknown in the pleasant familiar land; there is no fierce harsh sound there, but sweet music striking the ear.

Without sorrow, without grief, without death, without any sickness, without weakness, that is the character of Emhaim; such a marvel is rare.

Loveliness of a wondrous land, whose aspects are beautiful, whose view is fair, excellent; incomparable is its haze.

Then if one sees Airgthech, on which dragon-stones and crystals rain down, the sea makes the wave foam against the land, with crystal tresses from its mane.

Riches, treasures of every colour are in Cíuin, have they not been found? Listening to sweet music, drinking choice wine.

Golden chariots race across the plain of the sea rising with the tide to the sun; chariots of silver in Magh Mon, and of bronze without blemish.

Horses of golden yellow there on the meadow, other horses of purple colour; other noble horses beyond them, of the colour of the all-blue sky.

There comes at sunrise a fair man who lights up the level lands, he strides over the bright plain which the sea washes so that it becomes blood.

There comes a host across the clear sea, to the land they display their rowing; then they row to the bright stone from which a hundred songs arise.

Through the long ages it sings a melody which is not sad; the music swells up in choruses of hundreds, they do not expect decay nor death.

Emhnae of many shapes, beside the sea, whether it is near or whether it is far, where there are many thousands of motley-dressed women; the pure sea surrounds it.

If one has heard the sound of the music, the song of little birds from Imchíuin, a troop of women comes from the hill to the playing-field where it is.

Holiday-making and health come to the land around which laughter echoes; in Imchíuin with its purity come immortality and joy.

Through the perpetual good weather silver rains on
the lands; a very white cliff under the glare of the sea,
over which its heat spreads from the sun.

The host rides across Magh Mon, a lovely sport
which is not weakly; in the many-coloured land with
great splendour they do not expect decay nor death.

Listening to music in the night, and going to
Ildathach the many-coloured land, a brilliance with
clear splendour from which the white cloud glistens.

Anon. Seventh/Eighth century Irish
(transl. V. H. Jackson)

Isn't it strange that mankind should be eternally restless and
always aspiring to something—God knows what?

The Russians, who are a soulful people if given half a
chance, have a word for it—*stremldyniye*—meaning a
yearning, striving or longing for something. It runs through
Tchaikovsky's music and Keats's poetry for that matter too. I
wonder how a confirmed atheist explains it? Thomas Chalmers, a Scottish theologian of the first half of the nineteenth
century, had no doubts.

What meaneth this restlessness of our nature? What
meaneth this unceasing activity which longs for
exercise and employment, even after every object is
gained which first roused it to enterprise? What mean
those unmeasurable longings which no gratification
can extinguish, and which still continue to agitate the
heart of man, even in the fullness of plenty and of
enjoyment? If they mean anything at all, they mean
that all which this world can offer is not for him and he
is born for something beyond it—that the scene of his
earthly existence is too limited and he is formed to
expatiate in a wider and grander theatre—that a nobler
destiny is reserved for him—and that to accomplish
the purpose of his being he must soar above the
littleness of the world and aim at a loftier prize.

It forms the peculiar honour and excellence of
religion that it accommodates to this property of our
nature—that it holds out a prize suited to our high
calling—that there is a grandeur in its objects which

can fill and surpass the imagination—that it reveals
to the eye of faith the glories of an imperishable
world—and how from the high eminencies of heaven
a great cloud of witnesses are looking down upon
earth, not as a scene for the petty anxieties of time,
but as a splendid theatre for the ambition of
immortal spirits.

Thomas Chalmers (1780–1847) : 'Commercial Discourses

Seek, and ye shall find.

The Sermon on the Mount : Matthew 7 :

Tolstoy writes here unforgettably about his conversion, after
he'd sunk to the lowest depths of despair.

Five years ago I came to believe in Christ's teaching,
and my life suddenly changed; I ceased to desire what
I had previously desired, and began to desire what I
formerly did not want. What had previously seemed
to me good seemed evil, and what had seemed evil
seemed good. It happened to me as it happens to a
man who goes out on some business and on the way
suddenly decides that the business is unnecessary and
returns home. All that was on his right is now on his
left, and all that was on his left is now on his right;
his former wish to get as far as possible from home
has changed into a wish to be as near as possible to
it. The direction of my life and my desires became
different, and good and evil changed places. . . .
I, like that thief of the cross, have believed Christ's
teaching and been saved. And this is no far-fetched
comparison, but the closest expression of the condition of spiritual despair and horror at the problem of
life and death in which I lived formerly, and of the
condition of peace and happiness in which I am now.
I, like the thief, knew that I had lived and was living
badly. . . . I, like the thief, knew that I was unhappy
and suffering. . . . I, like the thief to the cross, was
nailed by some force to that life of suffering and evil.
And as, after the meaningless sufferings and evils of
life, the thief awaited the terrible darkness of death,
so did I await the same thing.

In all this I was exactly like the thief, but the difference was that the thief was already dying, while I was still living. The thief might believe that his salvation lay there beyond the grave, but I could not be satisfied with that, because besides a life beyond the grave life still awaited me here. But I did not understand that life. It seemed to me terrible. And suddenly I heard the words of Christ and understood them, and life and death ceased to seem to me evil, and instead of despair I experienced happiness and the joy of life undisturbed by death.

Leo Tolstoy (1828–1910): 'What I Believe'

Let not your heart be troubled: Ye believe in God, believe also in me. In my Father's house are many mansions: if it were not so I would have told you. I go to prepare a place for you. And if I go and prepare a place for you, I will come again, and receive you unto myself; that where I am, there ye may be also. And whither I go ye know, and the way ye know. Thomas saith unto him, Lord, we know not whither thou goest; and how can we know the way? Jesus saith unto him, I am the way, the truth and the life: no man cometh unto the Father, but by me. If ye had known me, ye should have seen my Father also: and from henceforth ye know him, and have seen him.

John 14 : 1

In our lives we all influence others and are influenced by them probably more than we know. Listen to the voice of a great prophet of our century.

One other thing stirs me when I look back at my youthful days, viz. the fact that so many people gave me something or were something to me without knowing it. Such people, with whom I never perhaps exchanged a word, yet, and others about whom I merely heard things by report, had a decisive influence on me; they entered into my life and became powers within me. Much that I should otherwise not have felt so clearly or done so effectively was felt or done as it was, because I stand, as it were, under the sway of these people. Hence I always think that we all live, spiritually, by what others have given us in the significant hours of our life. These significant hours do not announce themselves as coming, but arrive unexpected. Nor do they make a great show of themselves; they pass almost unperceived. Often, indeed, their significance comes home to us first as we look back, just as the beauty of a piece of music or of a landscape often strikes us first in our recollection of it. Much that has become our own in gentleness, modesty, kindness, willingness to forgive, in veracity, loyalty, resignation under suffering, we owe to people in whom we have seen or experienced these virtues at work, sometimes in a great matter, sometimes in a small. A thought which had become act sprang into us like a spark, and lighted a new flame within us. . . .

If we had before us those who have thus been a blessing to us, and could tell them how it came about, they would be amazed to learn what passed over from their life into ours.

Albert Schweitzer (1875–1965) : *'Memories
from Childhood and Youth'*

Robert Payne in his book *Schweitzer, Hero of Africa* writes of him as a boy:

In the evenings, after praying with his mother, he would add his own silent prayer for all living creatures: 'Dear God, protect and bless all things that breathe, guard them from all evil and let them sleep in peace.'

Sometimes the fact of pain shocked him into violent and repeated resolves to so order his life that he would inflict no pain on anything that lived and breathed. . . . When he was seven or eight he went out bird-hunting with a friend. Like his friend, he was armed with a catapult. At the moment when young Schweitzer stooped to gather a stone to insert in the catapult, the Easter bells rang out. It was like a sign from heaven. He began to shout and wave his arms, shooing the birds away, then he fled home. He had discovered the commandment that was to weigh increasingly on him over the years: 'Thou shalt not kill.' . . .

Ehrfurcht vor dem Leben. Reverence for Life. Ehrfurcht means more than 'reverence'. It has overtones of awe and shuddering wonder, and great blessedness. Before God a man may abase himself in holy awe. A man may humble himself before the infinite spaces of the firmament. So should a man humble himself before the ever-present miracle of life. Let him regard the miracle with reverential fear and wonder, and let him never cease regarding it in this way, for all life is the vehicle of the power of God. . . .

A man who possesses an entire veneration and awe of life will not simply say his prayers: he will throw himself into the battle to preserve life, if for no other reason than that he is himself an extension of the life around him, life being so holy and every man being part of this holiness. A man rejoicing in that veneration for life is therefore led 'into an unrest such as the world does not know, but he obtains from it a blessedness which the world cannot give'. And if his task is harder, because he assumes such huge responsibilities, the rewards are greater, for those who help to preserve life and heal wounds and diminish pain come to know the deepest happiness known to men.

Robert Payne

It's not difficult to agree with these words of Oliver Edwards, a friend of Boswell:

> I have tried too in my time to be a philosopher; but, I don't know how, cheerfulness was always breaking in.
>
> *Boswell's Dr Johnson, 17 April 1778*

If we may believe our logicians, man is distinguished from all other creatures by the faculty of laughter.

Joseph Addison (1672–1719)

MIRTH

'Tis mirth that fills the veins with blood,
More than wine, or sleep, or food;
Let each man keep his heart at ease;
No man dies of that disease!
He that would his body keep
From diseases, must not weep;
But whoever laughs and sings,
Never he his body brings
Into fevers, gouts, or rheums,
Or lingeringly his lungs consumes;
Or meets with ague in his bone,
Or catarrhs, or griping stone:
But contented lives for aye;
The more he laughs, the more he may!

?Francis Beaumont (?1584–1616)

Village cricket has probably inspired more laughter than most things. In *England, Their England* there is an all-time classic description of the final rites as the blacksmith, a demon bowler, prepares to polish off the tail of the 'Gents' team down from London. The scene—a village green in the 'Twenties.

It was the last ball of the over. He halted at the wicket before going back for his run, glared at Mr Harcourt, who had been driven out to umpire by his colleagues—greatly to the regret of Mr Bason, the landlord of the Shoes—glared at Mr Southcott, took another reef in his belt, shook out another inch in his braces, spat on his hand, swung his arm three or four times in a meditative sort of way, grasped the ball tightly in his colossal palm, and then turned smartly about and marched off like a Pomeranian grenadier and vanished over the brow of the hill. Mr Southcott, during these proceedings, leant elegantly upon his bat and admired the view. At last, after a long stillness, the ground shook, the grasses waved violently, small birds arose with shrill clamours, a loud puffing sound alarmed the butterflies, and the blacksmith, looking more like Venus Anadyomene than ever, came thundering over the crest. The world held its breath. Among the spectators conversation was suddenly hushed. Even the urchins, understanding somehow that they were assisting at a crisis in affairs, were silent for a moment as the mighty figure swept up to the crease. It was the charge of Von Bredow's Dragoons at Gravelotte over again.

But alas for human ambitions! Mr Harcourt, swaying slightly from leg to leg, had understood the menacing glare of the bowler, had marked the preparation for a titanic effort, and—for he was not a poet for nothing—knew exactly what was going on. And Mr Harcourt sober had a very pleasant sense of humour, but Mr Harcourt rather drunk was a perfect demon of impishness. Sober, he occasionally resisted a temptation to try to be funny. Rather drunk, never. As the giant whirlwind of vulcanic energy rushed past him to the crease, Mr Harcourt, quivering with excitement and internal laughter, and wobbling uncertainly upon his pins, took a deep breath and bellowed, 'No ball!'

It was too late for the unfortunate bowler to stop himself. The ball flew out of his hand like a bullet and hit third-slip, who was not looking, full pitch on the knee-cap. With a yell of agony third-slip began hopping about like a stork until he tripped over a tussock of grass and fell on his face in a bed of nettles, from which he sprang up again with another drum-splitting yell. The blacksmith himself was flung forward by his own irresistible momentum, startled out of his wits by Mr Harcourt's bellow in his ear, and thrown off his balance by his desperate effort to prevent himself from delivering the ball, and the result was that his gigantic feet got mixed up among each other and he fell heavily in the centre of the wicket, knocking up a cloud of dust and dandelion-seed and twisting his ankle. Rooks by hundreds arose in protest from the vicarage cedars. The urchins howled like intoxicated banshees. The gaffers gaped. Mr Southcott gazed modestly at the ground. Mr Harcourt gazed at the heavens. Mr Harcourt did not think the world had ever been, or could ever be again, quite such a capital place, even though he had laughed internally so much that he had got hiccups.

> Mr Hodge, emerging at that moment from the
> Three Horseshoes, surveyed the scene and then the
> scoreboard with an imperial air. Then he roared in
> the same rustic voice as before:
> 'You needn't play safe any more, Bob. Play your
> own game.'
> *A. G. MacDonell (1895–1941): 'England, Their England'*

Apart from the blacksmith, one of the central figures of a
village was, of course, the parson. To a certain extent he still
is although, nowadays, he usually has more than one village
to get round. This is a tribute to the 'reverend champion' of
the eighteenth-century village.

> Near yonder copse, where once the garden smiled,
> And still where many a garden-flower grows wild;
> There, where a few torn shrubs the place disclose,
> The village preacher's modest mansion rose.
> A man he was, to all the country dear,
> And passing rich with forty pounds a year;
> Remote from towns he ran his godly race,
> Nor e'er had changed, nor wished to change his place;
> Unpractised he to fawn, or seek for power,
> By doctrines fashioned to the varying hour;
> Far other aims his heart had learned to prize,
> More skilled to raise the wretched than to rise.
> His house was known to all the vagrant train,
> He chid their wanderings, but relieved their pain;
> The long-remembered beggar was his guest,
> Whose beard descending swept his aged breast;
> The ruined spendthrift, now no longer proud,
> Claim'd kindred there, and had his claims allowed;
> The broken soldier, kindly bade to stay,
> Sate by his fire, and talked the night away;
> Wept o'er his wounds, or, tales of sorrow done,
> Shouldered his crutch, and shewed how fields were
>   won.
> Pleased with his guests, the good man learned to
>   glow,
> And quite forgot their vices in their woe;
> Careless their merits, or their faults to scan,
> His pity gave ere charity began.

Thus to relieve the wretched was his pride,
And even his failings leaned to Virtue's side;
But in his duty prompt at every call,
He watched and wept, he prayed and felt, for all.
And, as a bird each fond endearment tries,
To tempt its new-fledged offspring to the skies;
He tried each art, reproved each dull delay,
Allured to brighter worlds, and led the way.
  Beside the bed where parting life was layed,
And sorrow, guilt, and pain, by turns, dismayed
The reverend champion stood. At his control,
Despair and anguish fled the struggling soul;
Comfort came down the trembling wretch to raise,
And his last faultering accents whispered praise.
  At church, with meek and unaffected grace,
His looks adorned the venerable place;
Truth from his lips prevailed with double sway,
And fools, who came to scoff, remained to pray.
The service past, around the pious man,
With steady zeal, each honest rustic ran;
Even children followed, with endearing wile,
And plucked his gown, to share the good man's smile.
His ready smile a parent's warmth exprest,
Their welfare pleased him, and their cares distrest;
To them his heart, his love, his griefs were given,
But all his serious thoughts had rest in Heaven.
As some tall cliff that lifts its awful form,
Swells from the vale, and midway leaves the storm,
Tho' round its breast the rolling clouds are spread,
Eternal sunshine settles on its head.
      Oliver Goldsmith (1730–1774): 'The Deserted Village'

Lawrence Hyde, at the time of the great depression in 1931,
wrote these words which are as apt today as they have ever
been.

> If anything in the nature of a religious revival ever
> takes place in this country . . . we shall be prudent not
> to expect the educated classes to play any more
> important a part in it than that which is played by
> people of quite humble origin and pretensions.
> Spiritual power, insight, and authority—these things

are apt at such an epoch to manifest themselves in the most unexpected places, to the confusion of the orthodox. A tram-driver who has been spiritually quickened in the way in which certain slaves were once quickened at the beginning of the Christian era, or as certain Quakers were quickened in the seventeenth century, is a figure to be reckoned with—particularly in a society which, like our own, is beginning to regard the capacities of its intelligentsia with distrust.

Lawrence Hyde : 'The Prospects of Humanism'

Thank God every morning when you get up that you have something to do which must be done, whether you like it or not. Being forced to work, and forced to do your best, will breed in you temperance, self-control, diligence, strength of will, content, and a hundred other virtues which the idle never know.

Charles Kingsley (1819–1875)

A good solid bit o' work lasts, if it's only laying a
　floor down.
Somebody's the better for it being done well, besides
　the man as does it.

(Source unknown)

The man that hath no music in himself
Nor is not mov'd with concord of sweet sounds,
Is fit for treasons, stratagems, and spoils;
The motions of his spirit are dull as night
And his affections dark as Erebus:
Let no such man be trusted.

William Shakespeare (1564–1616) :
'The Merchant of Venice'

Now some music which evokes the past.

KING'S COLLEGE CHAPEL

When to the music of Byrd or Tallis,
　The ruffed boys singing in the blackened stalls,
The candles lighting the small bones on their faces,
　The Tudors stiff in marble on the walls,

There comes to evensong Elizabeth or Henry,
   Rich with brocade, pearl, golden lilies, at the altar,
The scarlet lions leaping on their bosoms,
   Pale royal hands fingering the crackling psalter,

Henry is thinking of his lute and of backgammon,
   Elizabeth follows the waving song, the mystery,
Proud in her red wig and green jewelled favours;
   They sit in their white lawn sleeves, as cool as
      history.

Charles Causley (1917–)

An extract from a letter written by John Keats to a friend. At the time he was writing some of his finest poetry.

> ... I feel assured I should write from the mere yearning and fondness I have for the Beautiful even if my night's labours should be burnt every morning, and no eye ever shine upon them. But even now I am perhaps not speaking from myself, but from some character in whose soul I now live...

John Keats to Richard Woodhouse,
Tuesday 27 October, 1818

Sometimes, when I have writing to do or a speech to make I say a little prayer I thought up: 'Dear Lord, may my mind become as a blank page. Put the thoughts into my head, the words into my mouth and guide my pen, so that, in however infinitesimal a way, I may be used as an instrument for good.' The French theologian de Chardin expressed much the same thought only more beautifully:

> Try, with God's help, to perceive the connection—even physical and natural—which binds your labour with the building of the Kingdom of Heaven; try to realise that heaven itself smiles upon you and, through your works, draws you to itself; then, as you leave church for the noisy streets, you will remain with only one feeling, that of continuing to immerse yourself in God.

Pierre Teilhard de Chardin (1881–1955):
'Le Milieu Divin'

The books of the Apocrypha were excluded from the Old Testament at the time of the Reformation. They were thought to have no well-grounded claim to inspired authorship. All the same, they contain some beautiful writing and much wisdom. This extract is in praise of famous men and equally of those who have no memorial.

> Let us now praise famous men, and our fathers that begat us.
> The Lord hath wrought great glory by them through his great power from the beginning.
> Such as did bear rule in their kingdoms, men renowned for their power, giving counsel by their understanding, and declaring prophecies:
> Leaders of the people by their counsels, and by their knowledge of learning meet for the people, wise and eloquent in their instructions:
> Such as found out musical tunes, and recited verses in writing:
> Rich men furnished with ability, living peaceably in their habitations:
> All these were honoured in their generations, and were the glory of their times.
> There be some of them, that have left a name behind them, that their praises might be reported.
> And some there be, which have no memorial, who are finished, as though they had never been; and are become as though they had never been born; and their children after them.
> But these were merciful men, whose righteousness hath not been forgotten. . . . Their bodies are buried in peace; but their name liveth for evermore.
> The people will tell of their wisdom, and the congregation will shew forth their praise . . . but . . . how can he get wisdom that holdeth the plough, and that glorieth in the goad, that driveth oxen, and is occupied in their labours, and whose talk is of bullocks?
> He giveth his mind to make furrows; and is diligent to give the kine fodder.
> So every carpenter and workmaster, that laboureth

night and day: and they can cut and grave seals,
and are diligent to make great variety, and give
themselves to counterfeit imagery, and watch to
finish a work:

The smith also sitting by the anvil and considering
the iron work, the vapour of the fire wasteth his
flesh, and he fighteth with the heat of the furnace:
the noise of the hammer and the anvil is ever in
his ears, and his eyes still look upon the pattern of
the thing that he maketh; he setteth his mind to
finish his work, and watcheth to polish it perfectly:

So doth the potter sitting at his work, and turning
the wheel about with his feet, who is always carefully set at his work, and maketh all his work by
number;

He fashioneth the clay with his arm, and boweth
down his strength before his feet; he applieth himself to lead it over; and he is diligent to make clean
the furnace:

All these trust to their hands: and every one is wise
in his work.

Without these cannot a city be inhabited: and they
shall not dwell where they will, nor go up and
down:

They shall not be sought for in the publick counsel
nor sit high in the congregation: they shall not sit
on the judges' seat, nor understand the sentence
of judgment: they cannot declare justice and
judgment and they shall not be found where parables
are spoken.

But they will maintain the state of the world, and
(all) their desire is in the work of their craft.

The Apocrypha : The Book of Ecclesiasticus

Lord temper with tranquillity
Our manifold activity
That we may do our work for Thee
With very great simplicity.

(An old sixteenth-century prayer)

John Bunyan's wise and beautiful words which follow sound
very strange in our envy-ridden age.

Now as they were going along and talking, they espied a boy feeding his father's sheep. The boy was in very mean clothes, but of a very fresh and well-favoured countenance, and as he sate by himself he sang. Hark, said Mr Greatheart, to what the shepherd's boy saith. So they hearkened, and he said:

He that is down needs fear no fall,
　He that is low no pride:
He that is humble ever shall
　Have God to be his guide.

I am content with what I have,
　Little be it or much:
And, Lord, contentment still I crave,
　Because thou savest such.

Fullness to such a burden is
　That go on pilgrimage:
Here little, and hereafter bliss,
　Is best from age to age.

Then said their guide, Do you hear him? I will dare to say that this boy lives a merrier life, and wears more of that herb called hearts-ease in his bosom, than he that is clad in silk and velvet.

John Bunyan (1628–1688):
'The Pilgrim's Progress'

To be honest, to be kind—to earn a little and to spend a little less, to make upon the whole a family happier for his presence, to renounce when that shall be necessary and not to be embittered, to keep a few friends . . . above all . . . to keep friends with himself —here is a task for all that a man has of fortitude and delicacy.

Robert Louis Stevenson (1850–1894)

No man has ever owed more to his biographer than did Samuel Johnson to that indefatigable Scot James Boswell. For a moment let us attend them as the worthy Doctor airs his views.

On Tuesday, 26 July, I found Mr Johnson alone. It was a very wet day, and I again complained of the disagreeable effects of such weather. JOHNSON. 'Sir, this is all imagination, which physicians encourage; for man lives in air, as a fish lives in water; so that if the atmosphere press heavy from above, there is an equal resistance from below. To be sure, bad weather is hard upon people who are obliged to be abroad; and men cannot labour so well in the open air in bad weather, as in good: but, Sir, a smith or a taylor, whose work is within doors, will surely do as much in rainy weather, as in fair. Some very delicate frames, indeed, may be affected by wet weather; but not common constitutions.'

We talked of the education of children; and I asked him what he thought was best to teach them first. JOHNSON. 'Sir, it is no matter what you teach them first, any more than what leg you shall put into your breeches first. Sir, you may stand disputing which is best to put in first, but in the mean time your breech is bare. Sir, while you are considering which of two things you should teach your child first, another boy has learnt them both. . . .'

The conversation then took a philosophical turn. JOHNSON. 'Human experience, which is constantly contradicting theory, is the great test of truth. A system, built upon the discoveries of a great many minds, is always of more strength than what is produced by the mere workings of any one mind. There is not so poor a book in the world that would not be a prodigious effort were it wrought out entirely by a single mind, without the aid of prior investigators. . . .'

'As to the Christian religion, Sir, besides the strong evidence which we have for it, there is a balance in its favour from the number of great men who have been convinced of its truth, after a serious consideration of the question.'

James Boswell (1740–1795): 'Life of Johnson'

Napoleon Bonaparte, in his exile, once testified: 'Charlemagne, Alexander the Great, and I, founded great empires upon force, and here is One who founded an empire upon love. And now I am alone and forsaken, and there are millions who would die for Him.'

> Health is the greatest of gifts,
>   content the best riches;
> Trust is the best of relatives;
>   perfect repose is the highest happiness.
>
> *(Japanese saying)*

PAX

> All that matters is to be at one with the living God
> to be a creature in the house of the God of Life.
>
> Like a cat asleep on a chair
> at peace, in peace
> and at one with the master of the house, with the
>   mistress,
> at home, at home in the house of the living,
> sleeping on the hearth, and yawning before the fire.
>
> Sleeping on the hearth of the living world,
> yawning at home before the fire of life
> feeling the presence of the living God
> like a great reassurance
> a deep calm in the heart
> a presence
> as of a master sitting at the board
> in his own and greater being,
> in the house of life.
>
> *D. H. Lawrence (1885–1930)*

At a time when the reserves of Christian capital are running low, it is well to acknowledge the immense influence that the belief has had on our world. We would do well to remember too that if God is dead then everything is permitted—to the omnipotent State.

Is that really the new religion we want?

Talleyrand, of course, was the French Foreign Minister and represented France at the Congress of Vienna in 1814–15.

M. Lepeaux on one occasion confided to Talleyrand his disappointment at the ill success with which he had met in his attempt to bring into vogue a new religion which he regarded as an improvement on Christianity. He explained that despite all the efforts of himself and his supporters his propaganda made no way. He asked Talleyrand's advice as to what he was to do. Talleyrand replied that it was indeed difficult to found a new religion, more difficult indeed than could be imagined, so difficult that he hardly knew what to advise. 'Still', he said—after a moment's reflection, 'there is one plan which you might at least try. I should recommend you to be crucified and to rise again on the third day.'

Whether we are prepared or no to accept the occurrence of the Resurrection as a fact of history, we cannot deny the influence which a belief in it has exercised in the world. We cannot deny that it has brought life and immortality to light as no other belief could conceivably have done; that it has substituted for the fear of death, for a large portion of the human race, that sure and certain knowledge of God which is eternal life; that it has permeated our customs, our literature, and our language with a glory and a hope which could have been derived from no other source.

C. H. Robinson : 'Studies in the Resurrection of Christ'

Although sometimes it might appear that the dark ages are closing in on us again, there may yet be light. William Cowper may have felt much as we do when he wrote this famous hymn. And that was in 1779.

LIGHT SHINING OUT OF DARKNESS

God moves in a mysterious way
   His wonders to perform;
He plants his footsteps in the sea,
   And rides upon the storm.

Deep in unfathomable mines
   Of never-failing skill

He treasures up his bright designs,
    And works his sovereign will.

Ye fearful saints fresh courage take;
    The clouds ye so much dread
Are big with mercy, and shall break
    In blessings on your head.

Judge not the Lord by feeble sense,
    But trust him for his grace;
Behind a frowning providence
    He hides a smiling face.

His purposes will ripen fast
    Unfolding every hour;
The bud may have a bitter taste,
    But sweet will be the flower.

Blind unbelief is sure to err,
    And scan his work in vain;
God is his own interpreter,
    And he will make it plain.

William Cowper (1731–1800)

I am sure I have always thought of Christmas time,
when it came round—apart from the veneration due
to its sacred name and origin, if anything belonging
to it can be apart from that—as a good time, a kind,
forgiving, charitable, pleasant time—and I say, God
Bless it!

Charles Dickens (1812–1870)

A CHRISTMAS CAROL

In the bleak mid-winter
    Frosty wind made moan,
Earth stood hard as iron,
    Water like a stone;
Snow had fallen, snow on snow,
    Snow on snow,
In the bleak mid-winter
    Long ago.

Our God, Heaven cannot hold him,
  Nor earth sustain;
Heaven and earth shall flee away
  When he comes to reign:
In the bleak mid-winter
  A stable-place sufficed
The Lord God Almighty
  Jesus Christ.

Enough for him whom cherubim
  Worship night and day,
A breastful of milk
  And a mangerful of hay;
Enough for him whom angels
  Fall down before,
The ox and ass and camel
  Which adore.

Angels and archangels
  May have gathered there,
Cherubim and seraphim
  Thronged the air,
But only his mother
  In her maiden bliss
Worshipped the Beloved
  With a kiss.

What can I give him,
  Poor as I am?
If I were a shepherd
  I would bring a lamb,
If I were a wise man
  I would do my part,—
Yet what I can I give him,
  Give my heart.

Christina Rossetti (1830–1894)

JOURNEY OF THE MAGI

'A cold coming we had of it,
Just the worst time of the year
For a journey, and such a long journey:

The ways deep and the weather sharp,
The very dead of winter.'
And the camels galled, sore-footed, refractory,
Lying down in the melting snow.
There were times we regretted
The summer palaces on slopes, the terraces,
And the silken girls bringing sherbet.
Then the camel men cursing and grumbling
And running away, and wanting their liquor and
    women,
And the night-fires going out, and the lack of shelters,
And the cities hostile and the towns unfriendly
And the villages dirty and charging high prices:
A hard time we had of it.
At the end we preferred to travel all night,
Sleeping in snatches,
With the voices singing in our ears, saying
That this was all folly.

Then at dawn we came down to a temperate valley,
Wet, below the snow line, smelling of vegetation,
With a running stream and a water-mill beating the
    darkness,
And three trees on the low sky.
And an old white horse galloped away in the meadow.
Then we came to a tavern with vine-leaves over the
    lintel,
Six hands at an open door dicing for pieces of silver,
And feet kicking the empty wine-skins.
But there was no information, so we continued
And arrived at evening, not a moment too soon
Finding the place; it was (you may say) satisfactory.

All this was a long time ago, I remember,
And I would do it again, but set down
This set down
This: were we led all that way for
Birth or Death? There was a Birth, certainly,
We had evidence and no doubt. I had seen birth and
    death,
But had thought they were different; this Birth was
Hard and bitter agony for us, like Death, our death.

We returned to our places, these Kingdoms,
But no longer at ease here, in the old dispensation,
With an alien people clutching their gods.
I should be glad of another death.

T. S. Eliot (1888–1965)

There have been few more saintly figures than Martin Luther King Jr, the Negro Civil Rights leader. A light went out in the world when he was assassinated in 1968.

He was a man in the tradition of the great army of Christian martyrs down the ages.

Some of my personal sufferings over the last few years have also served to shape my thinking. I always hesitate to mention these circumstances for fear of conveying the wrong impression. A person who constantly calls attention to his trials and sufferings is in danger of developing a martyr complex and of making others feel that he is consciously seeking sympathy. It is possible for one to be self-centred in his self-denial and self-righteous in his self-sacrifice. But I feel somewhat justified in mentioning them in this article because of the influence they have had in shaping my thinking.

Due to my involvement in the struggle for the freedom of my people, I have known very few quiet days in the last few years. I have been arrested five times and put in Alabama jails. My home has been bombed twice. A day seldom passes that my family and I are not the recipients of threats of death. I have been the victim of a near-fatal stabbing. So in a real sense I have been battered by the storms of persecution. I must admit that at times I have felt that I could no longer bear such a heavy burden, and have been tempted to retreat to a more quiet and serene life. But every time such a temptation appeared, something came to strengthen and sustain my determination. I have learned now that the Master's burden is light precisely when we take his yoke upon us.

My personal trials have also taught me the value of

27

unmerited suffering. As my sufferings mounted I soon realised that there were two ways that I could respond to my situation: either to react with bitterness or seek to transform the suffering into a creative force. Recognising the necessity for suffering I have tried to make of it a virtue. If only to save myself from bitterness, I have attempted to see my personal ordeals as an opportunity to transform myself and heal the people involved in the tragic situation which now obtains. I have lived these last few years with the conviction that unearned suffering is redemptive.

There are some who still find the cross a stumbling block, and others consider it foolishness, but I am more convinced than ever before that it is the power of God unto social and individual salvation. So like Apostle Paul I can now humbly yet proudly say, 'I bear in my body the marks of the Lord Jesus'. The suffering and agonising moments through which I have passed over the last few years have also drawn me closer to God. More than ever before I am convinced of the reality of a personal God.

Martin Luther King Jr (1929–1968)

Mother Theresa who for years has been a Christ-like figure in the Calcutta slums is another light of the world. These are three of her prayers.

ON SILENCE

We need to find God, and he cannot be found in noise and restlessness. God is the friend of silence. See how nature—trees, flowers, grass—grow in silence; see the stars, the moon and sun, how they move in silence. Is not our mission to give God to the poor in the slums? Not a dead God, but a living, loving God. The more we receive in silent prayer, the more we can give in our active life. We need silence to be able to touch souls. The essential thing is not what we say, but what God says to us and through us. All our words will be useless unless they come from within— words which do not give the light of Christ increase the darkness.

ON HUMILITY

Let there be no pride or vanity in the work. The work is God's work, the poor are God's poor. Put yourself completely under the influence of Jesus, so that he may think his thoughts in your mind, do his work through your hands, for you will be all-powerful with him who strengthens you.

ON SUBMISSION

Make sure that you let God's grace work in your souls by accepting whatever he gives you, and giving him whatever he takes from you.

True holiness consists in doing God's will with a smile.

I compiled this anthology in the bicentennial year of the independence of the United States of America. It is good to remember the ideals, the courage and the faith that those Pilgrim Fathers carried with them from these shores across the Atlantic.

Francis Brett Young wrote his poem 'The Island' during our darkest days of the last war. These very same qualities were shown by the Americans when they returned to fight by our side.

ATLANTIC CHARTER

What were you carrying, Pilgrims, Pilgrims?
What did you carry beyond the sea?
We carried the Book, we carried the Sword,
A steadfast heart in the fear of the Lord,
And a living faith in His plighted word
That all men should be free.

What were your memories, Pilgrims, Pilgrims?
What of the dreams you bore away?
We carried the songs our fathers sung
By the hearths of home when they were young,
And the comely words of the mother-tongue
In which they learnt to pray.

29

What did you find there, Pilgrims, Pilgrims?
What did you find beyond the waves?
> *A stubborn land and a barren shore,*
> *Hunger and want and sickness sore;*
> *All these we found and gladly bore*
> *Rather than be slaves.*

How did you fare there, Pilgrims, Pilgrims?
What did you build in that stubborn land?
> *We felled the forest and tilled the sod*
> *Of a continent no man had trod*
> *And we established there, in the Grace of God,*
> *The rights whereby we stand.*

What are you bringing us, Pilgrims, Pilgrims?
Bringing us back in this bitter day?
> *The selfsame things we carried away;*
> *The book, The Sword,*
> *The fear of the Lord,*
> *And the boons our fathers dearly bought:*
> *Freedom of Worship, Speech and Thought,*
> *Freedom from Want, Freedom from Fear,*
> *The Liberties we hold most dear,*
> *And who shall say us Nay?*
>
> Francis Brett Young (1884–1954): from 'The Island'

Phillips Brooks was an American preacher who became Bishop
of Massachusetts in 1891. He reminded his congregation that
they were taking part in a long tradition of struggle between
good and evil.

> 'It is written, Man shall not live by bread alone.'
> What a man finds in his own consciousness, he is
> strengthened by being able to recognize in the whole
> history of his race. 'It is written' long ago, this which
> he is doing now. He is only tracing over with his
> blood the unfaded characters which other men have
> written in theirs. It is not a mere whim of his, this
> conviction that it is better to serve God than to eat
> bread. It is the corporate conviction of mankind.
> That is a very mysterious support, but it is a very

real one. It plants the weak tree of your will or mine into the rich soil of humanity. Do not lose that strength. Do not so misread history that it shall seem to you when you try to do right as if you were the first man that ever tried it. Put yourself with your weak little struggle into the company of all the strugglers in all time. Recognize in your little fight against your avarice, or your untruthfulness, or your laziness, only one skirmish in that battle whose field covers the earth, and whose clamour rises and falls from age to age, but never wholly dies. See in the perpetual struggle of good and evil that the impulse after good is eternal, and the higher needs are always asserting their necessity. In their persistent assertion read the prophecy of their final success and take courage.

Phillips Brooks (1835–1893) : 'Sermons, Vol. I'

The great nineteenth-century American essayist Ralph Waldo Emerson had no doubts. Incidentally, if you play Scrabble the word 'marplot' may be a winner. It means: 'One who mars or defects a plot or design by officious interference.'

A little consideration of what takes place around us every day would shew us that a higher law than that of our will regulates events; that our painful labours are very unnecessary, and altogether fruitless; that only in our easy, simple, spontaneous action are we strong, and by contenting ourselves with obedience we become divine. Belief and love,—a believing love will relieve us of a vast load of care. O my brothers, God exists. There is a soul at the centre of nature, and over the will of every man, so that none of us can wrong the universe. It has so infused its strong enchantment into nature, that we prosper when we accept its advice; and when we struggle to wound its creatures, our hands are glued to our sides, or they beat our own breasts. The whole course of things goes to teach us faith. We need only obey. There is guidance for each of us, and by lowly listening we shall hear the right word. Why need you choose so painfully your place, and occupation, and associates, and modes of action and of entertainment? Certainly there is a possible right for you, that precludes the need of balance and wilful election. For you there is a reality, a fit place and congenial duties. Place yourself in the middle of the stream of power and wisdom which flows into you as life, place yourself in the full centre of that flood, then you are without effort impelled to truth, to right, and a perfect contentment. Then you put all gainsayers in the wrong. Then you are the world, the measure of right, of truth, of beauty. If we will not be marplots with our miserable interferences, the work, the society, letters, arts, science, religion of men, would go on far better than now; and the Heaven predicted from the beginning of the world, and still predicted from the bottom of the heart, would organise itself, as do now the rose and the air and the sun.

Ralph Waldo Emerson (1803–1882): 'Essays'

It is interesting that when Emerson visited this country in 1847 he had this to say:

'So . . . I feel in regard to this aged England . . . pressed upon by transitions of trade and . . . competing populations—I see her not dispirited, not weak, but well remembering that she has seen dark days before;—indeed, with a kind of instinct that she sees a little better in a cloudy day, and that, in storm of battle and calamity, she has a secret vigour and a pulse like a cannon.'

I wonder how our pulse rates today!

Walt Whitman was much influenced by Emerson and shared his certitude.

MIRACLES

As to me I know of nothing else but miracles,
Whether I walk the streets of Manhatten,

Or dart my sight over the roofs of houses toward the
    sky,
Or wade with naked feet along the beach just in the
    edge of the water,
Or stand under trees in the woods,
Or talk by day with any one I love,
Or sit at table at dinner with the rest,
Or look at strangers opposite me riding in the car,
Or watch honey bees busy around the hive of a
    summer forenoon,
Or animals feeding in the fields,
Or birds, or the wonderfulness of insects in the air,
Or the wonderfulness of the sundown, or of stars
    shining so quiet and bright,
Or the exquisite delicate thin curve of the new moon
    in spring;
These with the rest, one and all, are to me miracles.

                        Walt Whitman (1819–1892)

e. e. cummings, the American lyric poet who died in 1962,
favoured an eccentric typography and punctuation. But he
too believed in miracles.

i am a little church (no great cathedral)
far from the splendor and squalor of hurrying cities
—i do not worry if briefer days grow briefest,
i am not sorry when sun and rain make april

my life is the life of the reaper and the sower;
my prayers are prayers of earth's own clumsily
    striving
(finding and losing and laughing and crying) children
whose any sadness or joy is my grief or my gladness

around me surges a miracle of unceasing
birth and glory and death and resurrection:
over my sleeping self float flaming symbols
of hope, and i wake to a perfect patience of mountains

i am a little church (far from the frantic
world with its rapture and anguish) at peace with
    nature

—i do not worry if longer nights grow longest;
i am not sorry when silence becomes singing

winter by spring, i lift my diminutive spire to
merciful Him Whose only now is forever:
standing erect in the deathless truth of His presence
(welcoming humbly His light and proudly His darkness)

e. e. cummings (1894–1962)

It was thought until recently that the following words had
been found in the Old St Paul's Church in Baltimore, Mary-
land. The author was said to be one of the early settlers in the
seventeenth century. We now know that they were written
by a Baltimore lawyer, Max Ehrmann, in 1927.

This does not in the least alter the fact that they are words
of great simplicity and wisdom: they are guide lines for a
happy life.

DESIDERATA

Go placidly amid the noise and haste, and remember
what peace there may be in silence. As far as possible
without surrender, be on good terms with all persons.
Speak your truth quietly and clearly; and listen to
others, even the dull and ignorant; they, too, have
their story. Avoid loud and aggressive persons, they
are vexatious to the spirit.

If you compare yourself with others, you may
become vain and bitter; for always there will be
greater and lesser persons than yourself. Enjoy your
achievements as well as your plans. Keep interested
in your own career, however humble; it is a real
possession in the changing fortunes of time. Exercise
caution in your business affairs; for the world is full
of trickery. But let this not blind you to what virtue
there is; many persons strive for high ideals; and
everywhere life is full of heroism.

Be yourself. Especially, do not feign affection.
Neither be cynical about love; for in the face of all
disenchantment it is perennial as the grass. Take

kindly the counsel of the years, gracefully surrender-
ing the things of youth. Nurture strength of spirit to
shield you in misfortune. But do not distress yourself
with imaginings. Many fears are born of fatigue and
loneliness. Beyond a wholesome discipline, be gentle
with yourself.

You are a child of the universe, no less than the
trees and the stars; you have a right to be here. And
whether or not it is clear to you, no doubt the universe is unfolding as it should. Therefore be at peace
with God, whatever you conceive him to be, and
whatever your labours and aspirations, in the noisy
confusion of life, keep peace with your soul.

With all its sham, drudgery and broken dreams, it is
still a beautiful world. Be careful. Strive to be happy.

The last word on 'The Spirit of Man' I leave to John Donne,
the greatest of English metaphysical poets. From 1621 to his
death ten years later he was Dean of St Paul's and frequently
preached before Charles I. His sermons were full of subtlety
and stand alone. This is one of the most famous passages.

No man is an island, entire of itself; every man is
a piece of the continent, a part of the main. If a clod
be washed away by the sea, Europe is the less, as well
as if a promontory were, as well as if a manor of thy
friend's or of thine own were; any man's death
diminishes me, because I am involved in mankind;
and therefore never send to know for whom the bell
tolls; it tolls for thee. Neither can we call this a
begging of misery, or a borrowing of misery, as
though we were not miserable enough of ourselves,
but must fetch in more from the next house, in taking
upon us the misery of our neighbours. Truly it were
an excusable covetousness if we did, for affliction is a
treasure, and scarce any man has enough of it. No
man hath affliction enough that is not matured and
ripened by it, and made fit for God by that affliction.
If a man carry treasure in bullion, or in a wedge of
gold, and have none coined into current money, his
treasure will not defray him as he travels. Tribula-

tion is treasure in the nature of it, but it is not current money in the use of it, except as we get nearer and nearer our home, heaven, by it. Another man may be sick too, and sick to death, and this affliction may lie in his bowels, as gold in a mine, and be of no use to him; but this bell, that tells me of his affliction, digs out and applies that gold to me: if by this consideration of another's danger I take mine own into contemplation, and so secure myself, by making my recourse to my God, who is our only security.

John Donne (1571 or 2-1631):
'Devotions upon Emergent Occasions', xvii

God be in my head,
  And in my understanding;
God be in my mouth,
  And in my speaking;
God be in my heart,
  And in my thinking.

Sarum Primer (1558)

SECTION TWO

SECTION TWO

SOME MANNER OF JOY

We set out in the company of Walt Whitman, the great
American nature poet and champion of his country's intellectual independence.

SONG OF THE OPEN ROAD

Afoot and light-hearted I take to the open road,
Healthy, free, the world before me,
The long brown path before me leading wherever I
    choose.

Henceforth I ask not good-fortune, I myself am good-
    fortune,

Henceforth I whimper no more, postpone no more,
    need nothing,
Done with indoor complaints, libraries, querulous
    criticisms,
Strong and content I travel the open road.

The earth, that is sufficient,
I do not want the constellations any nearer,
I know they are very well where they are,
I know they suffice for those who belong to them. . . .

You road I enter upon and look around, I believe you
    are not all that is here,
I believe that much unseen is also here.

> *Walt Whitman (1819–1892) : 'Leaves of Grass'*

This may not be one of Keats's greatest poems but for me it
spells Hampstead Heath. Keats was essentially a Hampstead
man and even today there are many parts of the Heath and
Old Hampstead where he would feel at home. His house in
Keats Grove has become a shrine visited by thousands of
tourists every year. Sadly though, the nightingale sings no
more.

NATURE'S ENCHANTMENT

To one who has been long in city pent,
    'Tis very sweet to look into the fair
    And open face of heaven,—to breathe a prayer
Full in the smile of the blue firmament.
Who is more happy, when, with heart's content,
    Fatigued he sinks into some pleasant lair
    Of wavy grass, and reads a debonair
And gentle tale of love and languishment?
Returning home at evening, with an ear
    Catching the notes of Philomel,—an eye
Watching the sailing cloudlet's bright career,
    He mourns that day so soon has glided by,
E'en like the passage of an angel's tear
    That falls through the clear ether silently.

> *John Keats (1795–1821)*

Here is a passage from *Bevis*, that immortal prose epic of boyhood, by the nineteenth-century nature mystic Richard Jefferies. He writes of the things that do not change: boyhood and nature.

> The heavens were as much a part of life as the elms, the oak, the house, the garden and orchard, the meadow and the brook. They were no more separated than the furniture of the parlour, than the old oak chair where he sat, and saw the new moon shine over the mulberry tree. They were neither above nor beneath, they were in the same place with him; just as when you walk in a wood the trees are all about you, on a plane with you, so he felt the constellations and the sun on a plane with him, and that he was moving among them as the earth rolled on, like them, with them, in the stream of space.
>
> The day did not shut off the stars, the night did not shut off the sun; they were always there. Not that he always thought of them, but they were never dismissed. When he listened to the greenfinches sweetly calling in the hawthorn, or when he read his books, poring over the Odyssey, with the sunshine on the wall, they were always there; there was no severance. Bevis lived not only out to the finches and the swallows, to the far-away hills, but he lived out and felt out to the sky.
>
> It was living, not thinking. He lived it, never thinking, as the finches live their sunny life in the happy days of June. There was magic in everything, blades of grass and stars, the sun and the stones upon the ground.
>
> The green path by the strawberries was the centre of the world, and round it by day and night the sun circled in a magical golden ring.
>
> *Richard Jefferies (1848–1887): 'Bevis'*

Tennyson, the great Victorian Poet Laureate, wrote some heavy-going stuff, but this poem has for me a simple perfection.

THE SHELL

See what a lovely shell,
Small and pure as a pearl,
Lying close to my foot,
Frail, but a work divine,
Made so fairily well
With delicate spire and whorl.
How exquisitely minute,
A miracle of design.

What is it? a learned man
Could give it a clumsy name.
Let him name it who can,
The beauty would be the same.

The tiny cell is forlorn,
Void of the little living will
That made it stir on the shore.
Did he stand at the diamond door
Of his house in a rainbow frill?
Did he push when he was uncurled
A golden foot or a fairy horn
Through his dim water world?

Slight, to be crushed with a tap
Of my finger-nail on the sand,
Small, but a work divine,
Frail, but of force to withstand,
Year upon year, the shock
Of cataract seas that snap
The three-decker's oaken spine
Athwart the ledges of rock
Here on the Breton strand!

Alfred Tennyson (1809–1892)

Bleak House is one of Dickens's more downbeat books, but
what a master of description he was: the magic of a moonlight night.

A very quiet night. When the moon shines very
brilliantly, a solitude and stillness seem to proceed

from her, that influence even crowded places full of life. Not only is it a still night on dusty high roads and on hill-summits, whence a wide expanse of country may be seen in repose, quieter and quieter as it spreads away into a fringe of trees against the sky, with the gray ghost of a bloom upon them; not only is it a still night in gardens and in woods, and on the river where the water-meadows are fresh and green, and the stream sparkles on among pleasant islands, murmuring weirs, and whispering rushes; not only does the stillness attend it as it flows where houses cluster thick, where many bridges are reflected in it, where wharves and shipping make it black and awful, where it winds from these disfigurements through marshes whose grim beacons stand like skeletons washed ashore, where it expands through the bolder region of rising grounds, rich in cornfield, windmill and steeple, and where it mingles with the ever-heaving sea; not only is it a still night on the deep, and on the shore where the watcher stands to see the ship with her spread wings cross the path of light that appears to be presented to only him; but even on this stranger's wilderness of London there is some rest. Its steeples and towers, and its one great dome, grow more ethereal; its smoky house-tops lose their grossness, in the pale effulgence; the noises that arise from the streets are fewer and are softened, and the footsteps on the pavements pass more tranquilly away. In these fields of Mr Tulkinghorn's inhabiting, where the shepherds play on Chancery pipes that have no stop, and keep their sheep in the fold by hook and by crook until they have shorn them exceeding close, every noise is merged, this moonlight night, into a distant ringing hum, as if the city were a vast glass, vibrating.

Charles Dickens (1812–1870): 'Bleak House'

In 1793 Wordsworth moved with his sister Dorothy to Somerset. Tintern Abbey is from his collection *Lyrical Ballads* which he published with his great friend Samuel Taylor Coleridge in 1798.

LINES COMPOSED A FEW MILES
ABOVE TINTERN ABBEY

                    The sounding cataract
Haunted me like a passion; the tall rock,
The mountain, and the deep and gloomy wood,
Their colours and their forms, were then to me
An appetite; a feeling and a love,
That had no need of a remoter charm,
By thought supplied, nor any interest
Unborrowed from the eye.—That time is past.
And all its aching joys are now no more,
And all its dizzy raptures. Not for this
Faint I, nor mourn, nor murmur; other gifts
Have followed; for such loss, I would believe,
Abundant recompense. For I have learned
To look on Nature, not as in the hour
Of thoughtless youth; but hearing oftentimes
The still, sad music of humanity,
Nor harsh, nor grating, though of ample power
To chasten and subdue. And I have felt
A presence that disturbs me with the joy
Of elevated thoughts; a sense sublime,
Of something far more deeply interfused,
Whose dwelling is the light of setting suns,
And the round ocean and the living air,
And the blue sky, and in the mind of man;
A motion and a spirit, that impels
All thinking things, all objects of all thought,
And rolls through all things. Therefore am I still
A lover of the meadows and the woods,
And mountains; and of all that we behold
From this green earth; of all the mighty world
Of eye and ear,—both what they half create,
And what perceive; well pleased to recognize
In nature and the language of the sense,
The anchor of my purest thoughts, the nurse,
The guide, the guardian of my heart, and soul
Of all my moral being.

                  William Wordsworth (*1770–1850*)

John Clare was an incomparable nature poet; his prose is less well known. How beautiful and serene is this passage. Nothing escapes the clarity of his vision.

DEWDROPS

The dewdrops on every blade of grass are so much like silver drops that I am obliged to stoop down as I walk to see if they are pearls, and those sprinkled on the ivy-woven beds of primroses underneath the hazels, whitethorns, and maples are so like gold beads that I stooped down to feel if they were hard, but they melted from my finger. And where the dew lies on the primrose, the violet and whitethorn leaves, they are emerald and beryl, yet nothing more than the dews of the morning on the budding leaves; nay, the road grasses are covered with gold and silver beads, and the further we go the brighter they seem to shine, like solid gold and silver. It is nothing more than the sun's light and shade upon them in the dewy morning; every thorn-point and every bramble-spear has its trembling ornament: till the wind gets a little brisker, and then all is shaken off, and all the shining jewelry passes away into a common spring morning full of budding leaves, primroses, violets, vernal speedwell, bluebell and orchids, and commonplace objects.

John Clare (1793–1864): Written in Northampton Asylum

This I love. A night of such beauty that even the horses should be on tip-toe.

NIGHT OF SPRING

Slow, horses, slow,
As through the woods we go—
We would count the stars in heaven,
Hear the grasses grow:

Watch the cloudlets few
Dappling the deep blue,
In our open palms outspread
Catch the blessed dew.

Slow, horses, slow,
As through the woods we go—
We would see fair Dian rise
With her huntress bow:

We would hear the breeze
Ruffling the dim trees,
Hear its sweet love-ditty set
To endless harmonies.

Slow, horses, slow,
As through the woods we go—
All the beauty of the night
We would learn and know!

Thomas Westwood (1814–1884)

George Meredith sings a paean of praise to early summer.

THE SWEET O' THE YEAR

Now the frog, all lean and weak,
  Yawning from his famished sleep,
Water in the ditch doth seek,
    Fast as he can stretch and leap:
      Marshy king-cups burning near
      Tell him 'tis the sweet o' the year.

Now the ant works up his mound
  In the mouldered piny soil,
And above the busy ground
    Takes the joy of earnest toil:
      Dropping pine-cones, dry and sere,
      Warn him 'tis the sweet o' the year.

Now the chrysalis on the wall
  Cracks, and out the creature springs,
Raptures in his body small,
    Wonders on his dusty wings:
      Bells and cups, all shining clear,
      Show him 'tis the sweet o' the year.

Now the brown bee, wild and wise,
  Hums abroad, and roves and roams,

Storing in his wealthy thighs
   Treasure for the golden combs:
     Dewy buds and blossoms dear
     Whisper 'tis the sweet o' the year.

Now the May-fly and the fish
   Play again from moon to night;
Every breeze begets a wish,
   Every motion means delight:
     Heaven high over heath and mere
     Crowns with blue the sweet o' the year.

Now all Nature is alive,
   Bird and beetle, man and mole;
Bee-like goes the human hive,
   Lark-like sings the soaring soul:
     Hearty faith and honest cheer
     Welcome in the sweet o' the year.

George Meredith (1828-1909)

Francis Bacon, the great Elizabethan philosopher and statesman, like many wise people loved gardens.

And because the breath of flowers is far sweeter in the air (where it comes and goes, like the warbling of music) than in the hand, therefore nothing is more fit for that delight, than to know what be the flowers and plants that do best perfume the air. Roses, damask and red, are fast flowers of their smells; so that you may walk by a whole row of them, and find nothing of their sweetness; yea, though it be in a morning's dew. Bays, likewise, yield no smell as they grow; rosemary little, nor sweet marjoram; that which, above all others, yields the sweetest smell in the air is the violet, specially the white double violet, which comes twice a year, about the middle of April, and about Bartholomew-tide. Next to that is the musk-rose; then the strawberry leaves dying with a most excellent cordial smell; then the flowers of the vines—it is a little dust, like the dust of a bent, which grown upon the cluster in the first coming forth. Then sweet briar; then wallflowers, which are

very delightful to set under a parlour or lower
chamber window; then pinks and gilliflowers,
specially the matted pink, and clove gilliflower; then
the flowers of the lime tree; then the honeysuckles,
so they be somewhat afar off. Of bean flowers I
speak not, because they are field flowers; but those
which perfume the air most delightfully, not passed
by as the rest, but being trodden upon and crushed
are three—that is burnet, wild thyme, and water
mints; therefore you are to set whole alleys of them,
to have the pleasure, when you walk or tread.

Francis Bacon (1561–1626): 'Of Gardens'

Many will agree that the greatest singer of all garden birds is
the blackbird. Len Howard, who was a professional musician
and spent her life with birds, getting to know them as indi-
viduals, maintained that they can compose. One of hers
composed a phrase almost identical with the opening phrase
of the *Rondo* in Beethoven's *Violin Concerto*. Here, R. S.
Thomas evokes magically the sound of the blackbird's song.

A BLACKBIRD SINGING

It seems wrong that out of this bird,
Black, bold, a suggestion of dark
Places about it, there yet should come
Such rich music, as though the notes'
Ore were changed to a rare metal
At one touch of that bright bill.

You have heard it often, alone at your desk
In a green April, your mind drawn
Away from its work by sweet disturbance
Of the mild evening outside your room.

A slow singer, but loading each phrase
With history's overtones, love, joy
And grief learned by his dark tribe
In other orchards and passed on
Instinctively as they are now,
But fresh always with new tears.

R. S. Thomas (1913–)

In Hardy's novels based in Dorset, the region he called Wessex, there are so many unforgettable descriptions of the countryside and its age-old customs. Here, the Maypole goes up on the edge of Egdon Heath.

Venn soon after went away, and in the evening Yeobright strolled as far as Fairway's cottage. It was a lovely May sunset, and the birch trees which grew on this margin of the vast Egdon wilderness had put on their new leaves, delicate as butterflies' wings, and diaphanous as amber. Beside Fairway's dwelling was an open space recessed from the road, and here were now collected all the young people from within a radius of a couple of miles. The pole lay with one end supported on a trestle, and women were engaged in wreathing it from the top downwards with wildflowers. The instincts of merry England lingered on here with exceptional vitality, and the symbolic customs which tradition has attached to each season of the year were yet a reality on Egdon. Indeed, the impulses of all such outlandish hamlets are pagan still: in these spots homage to nature, self-adoration, frantic gaieties, fragments of Teutonic rites to divinities whose names are forgotten, seem in some way or other to have survived mediaeval doctrine.

Yeobright did not interrupt the preparations, and went home again. The next morning, when Thomasin withdrew the curtains of her bedroom window, there stood the Maypole in the middle of the green, its top cutting into the sky. It had sprung up in the night, or rather early morning, like Jack's bean-stalk. She opened the casement to get a better view of the garlands and posies that adorned it. The sweet perfume of the flowers had already spread into the surrounding air, which, being free from every taint, conducted to her lips a full measure of the fragrance received from the spire of blossom in its midst. At the top of the pole were crossed hoops decked with small flowers; beneath these came a milk-white zone of Maybloom; then a zone of bluebells, then of cowslips, then of lilacs, then of ragged-robins, daffodils, and so on, till the lowest stage was reached. Thomasin

noticed all these, and was delighted that the May-
revel was to be so near.

Thomas Hardy (1840-1928): 'The Return of the Native

Robert Bridges remembers a walk on the South Downs.

Or as I well remember one highday in June
bright on the seaward South-downs, where I had com-
    afar
on a wild garden planted years agone, and fenced
thickly within live-beechen walls: the season it was
of prodigal gay blossom, and man's skill had made
a fair-order'd husbandry of that native pleasaunce:
But had there been no more than earth's wild love-
    liness,
the blue sky and the soft air and the unknown
    flowersprent lawns,
I would have lain me down and long'd, as then I did,
to lie there ever indolently undisturb'd, and watch
the common flowers that starr'd the fine grass of the
    wold,
waving in gay display their gold-heads to the sun,
each telling of its own inconscient happiness,
each type a faultless essence of God's will, such gems
as magic master-minds in painting or music
threw aside once for man's regard or disregard;
things supreme in themselves, eternal, unnumber'd
in the unexplored necessities of Life and Love.

Robert Bridges (1844-1930): 'The Testament of Beauty', I. 1

An extract now from a diary kept by a Japanese lady nearly
thousand years ago. She was a lady-in-waiting at the Heia
Court. Her name was Sei Shonagon and the book is unique i
Japanese literature.

During the hot months it is a great delight to sit on
the veranda, enjoying the cool of the evening and
observing how the outlines of objects gradually
become blurred. At such a moment I particularly
enjoy the sight of a gentleman's carriage, preceded
by outriders clearing the way. Sometimes a couple

of commoners will pass in a carriage with the rear blinds slightly raised. As the oxen trot along, one has a pleasant sense of freshness. It is still more delightful when the sound of a lute or flute comes from inside the carriage, and one feels sorry when it disappears in the distance. Occasionally one catches a whiff of the oxen's leather cruppers; it is a strange, unfamiliar smell, but, absurd as it may seem, I find something rather pleasant about it.

On a very dark night it is delightful when the aroma of smoke from the pine-torches at the head of a procession is wafted through the air and pervades the carriage in which one is travelling.

'The Pillow Book of Sei Shonagon'.
Transl. by Ivan Morris

D. H. Lawrence wrote this free verse poem while living in Sicily. It is immensely powerful imagery.

SNAKE

... Someone was before me at my water-trough,
And I, like a second comer, waiting.

He lifted his head from his drinking, as cattle do,
And looked at me vaguely, as drinking cattle do,
And flickered his two-forked tongue from his lips,
    and mused a moment,
And stooped and drank a little more,
Being earth-brown, earth-golden from the burning
    bowels of the earth
On the day of Sicilian July, with Etna smoking.

The voice of my education said to me
He must be killed,
For in Sicily the black, black snakes are innocent,
    the gold are venomous.

And voices in me said, If you were a man
You would take a stick, and break him now, and
    finish him off.

But must I confess how I liked him,
How glad I was he had come like a guest in quiet, to
    drink at my water-trough
And depart peaceful, pacified, and thankless,
Into the burning bowels of this earth?

Was it cowardice, that I dared not kill him?
Was it perversity, that I longed to talk to him?
Was it humility, to feel so honoured?
I felt so honoured.

And yet those voices:
If you were not afraid, you would kill him!

And truly I was afraid, I was most afraid,
But even so, honoured still more
That he should seek my hospitality
From out the dark door of the secret earth.

He drank enough
And lifted his head, dreamily, as one who has
    drunken,
And flickered his tongue like a forked night on the
    air, so black,
Seeming to lick his lips,
And looked around like a god, unseeing, into the air,
And slowly turned his head,
And slowly, very slowly, as if thrice adream,
Proceeded to draw his slow length curving round
And climb again the broken bank of my wall-face.

And as he puts his head into that dreadful hole,
And as he slowly drew up, snake-easing his shoulders,
    and entered farther,
A sort of horror, a sort of protest against his with-
    drawing into that horrid black hole,
Deliberately going into the blackness, and slowly
    drawing himself after,
Overcame me now his back was turned.

I looked around, I put down my pitcher,
I picked up a clumsy log
And threw it at the water-trough with a clatter.

I think it did not hit him,
But suddenly that part of him that was left behind
  convulsed in undignified haste,
Writhed like lightning, and was gone
Into the black hole, the earth-lipped fissure in the
  wall-front,
At which, in the intense still noon, I stared with
  fascination
...

And immediately I regretted it.
I thought how paltry, how vulgar, what a mean act!
I despised myself and the voices of my accursed
  human education.

And I thought of the albatross,
And I wished he would come back, my snake.

For he seemed to me again like a king,
Like a king in exile, uncrowned in the underworld,
Now due to be crowned again.

And so, I missed my chance with one of the lords
Of life.
And I have something to expiate;
A pettiness.

D. H. Lawrence (1885–1930)

Henry Williamson was another of our great nature writers and greatly influenced in his mystic approach by Richard Jefferies.

I was alone with the wheat that I loved. Moving over the field my feet were drenched in an instant by the dew. Lying at full length on the earth, I pressed my face among the sweet wistfulness of stalks, stained and glowing as with some lambent fire, pale, mysterious. On each pale flame-blade depended a small white light, a dew-drop in which the light of the moon was imprisoned. Each flag of wheat held the beauty of pure water, and within the sappy blades glowed the spirit of the earth—in the spectral silence a voice spoke of its ancient lineage: of the slow horses that

had strained to the wooden plough through the ages,
scarring the glebe in long furrows that must be sown
with corn; race after race of slow horses moving in
jangling harness to the deep shouts of the heavy men.
Generation after generation of men, bent with age and
unceasing labour, plodding the earth, sowing the yellow
grains that would produce a million million berries for
mankind.

Henry Williamson (1897–1977): 'The Lone Swallows'

Arthur Bryant writes of the way he used to get the harvest in,
when he owned a few hundred acres of Wiltshire valley and
woodland. He wrote this in 1949.

THE CORNFIELD

All afternoon and evening we worked in the cornfield,
stooking the crop which was to feed our little stock,
and so, indirectly, man, during the coming year. The
machines for cutting and binding had arrived late,
and several days of a week of sunshine had been lost
waiting for them; the air was translucent and the
distant horizon of cliffs and sea so beautiful that the
thought of rain was never far away. We therefore
worked urgently, following close in the sweeping
tracks of the binder, moving slowly in from the wide
circumference towards the narrowing heart of
shimmering corn. None of us, save the men on the
machines, were very experienced in the art, but,
knowing what depended on it, we worked with a will
and with that steady unceasing compulsion which all
work with living nature seems to necessitate. The
goal in our minds was not the hour at which labour
ceased, but the completion of the work, the last stook
stacked, the field clear and garnered. Even the beauty
of the scene was incidental. Only occasionally did we
raise our eyes from that high, slanting field, sparkling
and rustling in sun and wind, to take in the wonderful panorama below: the old grey house, with its
William and Mary red brick chimneys rising out of
the trees, the green clay pastures stretching to the
margin of the sea, and the tawny downs, the jagged

cliffs of shale, limestone and chalk spread in fantastic panorama from Broad Bench to Ringstead, the blue of Weymouth Bay and Portland lying like a distant giant floating on the bosom of the Channel, the high, white clouds driving like solitary galleons out of the west. No more beautiful setting to the husbandman's business can have ever existed, and, as the shadows lengthened and the rooks began to wheel home, its loveliness and peace surpassed the human power of description. Our throats and lips were parched, our feet battered by the iron, uneven ground, our bodies pierced with innumerable spear-points of oats and barley, but, as the corn vanished and the stooks rose, in sunlight, twilight and, last of all, in moonlight, a feeling of aching triumph and satisfaction overcame weariness. We had been all-day participants in a battle and it was nearly over. The enemy, next winter's want, on our little piece of the farming front—all that we could see and experience—was in retreat. A victory had been won.

Arthur Bryant (1899–) : 'The Lion and the Unicorn'

I cannot resist Hardy's famous sheep-shearing scene from *Far From the Madding Crowd.*

One could say about this barn, what could hardly be said of either the church or the castle, akin to it in age and style, that the purpose which had dictated its original erection was the same with that to which it was still applied. Unlike and superior to either of those two typical remnants of mediaevalism, the old barn embodied practices which had suffered no mutilation at the hands of time. Here at least the spirit of the ancient builders was at one with the spirit of the modern beholder. Standing before this abraded pile, the eye regarded its present usage, the mind dwelt upon its past history, with a satisfied sense of functional continuity throughout—a feeling almost of gratitude, and quite of pride, at the permanence of the idea which had heaped it up. The fact that four centuries had neither proved it to be founded on a mistake, inspired any hatred of its purpose, nor given rise to any reaction that had battered it down, invested this simple grey effort of old minds with a repose, if not a grandeur, which a too curious reflection was apt to disturb in its ecclesiastical and military compeers. For once mediaevalism and modernism had a common standpoint. The lanceolate windows, the time-eaten archstones and chamfers, the orientation of the axis, the misty chestnut work of the rafters, referred to no exploded fortifying art or worn-out religious creed. The defence and salvation of the body by daily bread is still a study, a religion, a desire.

Today the large side doors were thrown open towards the sun to admit a bountiful light to the immediate spot of the shearers' operations, which was the wood threshing-floor in the centre, formed of thick oak, black with age and polished by the beating of flails for many generations, till it had grown as slippery and as rich in hue as the stateroom floors of an Elizabethan mansion. Here the shearers knelt, the sun slanting in upon their bleached shirts, tanned arms, and the polished shears they flourished, causing them to bristle with a thousand rays strong enough to blind a weak-eyed man. Beneath them a captive sheep lay panting, quickening its pants as misgiving merged in terror, till it quivered like the hot landscape outside.

This picture of to-day with its frame of four hundred years ago did not produce that marked contrast between ancient and modern which is implied by the contrast of date. In comparison with cities Weatherbury was immutable. The citizen's *Then* is the rustic's *Now*. In London, twenty or thirty years ago are old times; in Paris ten years, or five; in Weatherbury three or four score years were included in the mere present, and nothing less than a century set a mark on its face or tone. Five decades hardly modified the cut of a gaiter, the embroidery of a smock-frock, by the breadth of a hair. Ten generations failed to alter the turn of a single phrase. In these Wessex nooks the busy outsider's ancient times are only old; his old times are still new; his present is futurity.

So the barn was natural to the shearers, and the shearers were in harmony with the barn.

Thomas Hardy (1840–1928): 'Far from the Madding Crowd'

Even if I were not an Autumn person I believe I would still think his 'Ode' the finest thing Keats ever wrote.

TO AUTUMN

Season of mists and mellow fruitfulness,
    Close bosom-friend of the maturing sun;
Conspiring with him how to load and bless
    With fruit the vines that round the thatch-eaves
            run;
To bend with apples the mossed cottage-trees,
    And fill all fruit with ripeness to the core;
        To swell the gourd, and plump the hazel shells
With a sweet kernel; to set budding more,
    And still more, later flowers for the bees,
    Until they think warm days will never cease;
        For Summer has o'erbrimmed their clammy
            cells.

Who hath not seen thee oft amid thy store?
    Sometimes whoever seeks abroad may find
Thee sitting careless on a granary floor,
    Thy hair soft-lifted by the winnowing wind;
Or on a half-reaped furrow sound asleep,
    Drowsed with the fume of poppies, while thy hook
        Spares the next swath and all its twinèd flowers;
And sometimes like a gleaner thou dost keep
    Steady thy laden head across a brook;
    Or by a cider-press, with patient look,
        Thou watchest the last oozings, hours by hours.

Where are the songs of Spring? Ay, where are they?
    Think not of them, thou hast thy music too, –
While barrèd clouds bloom the soft-dying day
    And touch the stubble-plains with rosy hue;
Then in a wailful choir the small gnats mourn
    Among the river sallows, borne aloft

> Or sinking as the light wind lives or dies;
> And full-grown lambs loud bleat from hilly bourn;
> Hedge-crickets sing; and now with treble soft
> The red-breast whistles from a garden-croft,
> And gathering swallows twitter in the skies.
>
> *John Keats (1795–182*

This will strike a chord with any of us who feed the birds i
winter.

ON A COLD DAY

> My sacrament of wine and broken bread
> Is now prepared, and ready to be done;
> The Tit shall hold a crust with both his feet,
> While, crumb by crumb, he picks it like a bone.
> The Thrush, ashamed of his thin ribs, has blown
> His feathers out, to make himself look fat;
> The Robin, with his back humped twice as high,
> For pity's sake—has crossed my threshold mat.
> The Sparrow's here, the Finch and Jenny Wren,
> The wine is poured, the crumbs are white and
> small—
> And when each little mouth has broken bread—
> Shall I not drink and bless them one and all?
>
> *W. H. Davies (1871–194*

Viscount Grey of Fallodon, the distinguished statesman—h
was Foreign Secretary from 1905 to 1916—was also a cor
siderable amateur naturalist. In particular he found birds, as h
put it, 'a pleasant path for recreation'. Indeed, his book *Th
Charm of Birds*, in which he wrote sensitively of the birds h
saw at his home in the north-east part of Northumberland, is
minor classic. I especially like this description.

> It was Christmas morning, many years ago when my
> sight was less impaired; the sun does not rise till
> after half-past eight in Northumberland at this
> season. I went out after breakfast; the waterfowl had
> been fed rather later than usual: they were still
> finishing their meal under the big larch tree or were

assembled at this end of the pond, which, being much shut in by trees and shrubs, was still in dark shadow. I went to the other pond some two hundred yards away and sat on the garden seat on the farther side. This pond is more open: there are no tall trees on the east side, and all the water was in full sunlight. There was not a bird on it; there was no stir in the air; the surface of the water was smooth and without motion. Presently pintail, wigeon, tufted ducks, pochards and one or two other kinds began to come flying over the intervening shrubs and trees from the pond where they had been fed. They came, some singly, some two or three together. None of them had yet seen the sun that morning, and each and all, as if in greeting to it, began to sport and play. They threw the water over their bodies, they raised themselves up on it and flapped their wings: they swam rapidly about in all directions, low in the water with quick and eager forward dartings of the head and neck. They sprang from the water into the air and took headers from the air into the water; they made short flights in one direction, lit on the water for a moment, and made another flight back in the direction whence they came; they dived unexpectedly, travelled under water, came up in some new place, and then, as if surprised at what they saw, dived again with exceeding suddenness. They splashed for the sake of splashing; there was not a square foot of water that was not in constant agitation. For some time the scene was one of motions of delight and exhilaration. At length first one bird and then another flew up on to the bank that faced the sun, or on to the south end of a little island; there they stood or sat, many of them side by side in pairs, and rested motionless or slept. Some half-dozen birds only remained on the water, and each of these was still, the head turned round and the bill resting in the feathers of the back. All was quiet; there was no sound or stir; the water was again smooth, the reflections in it were composed once more; the sun still shone; on the water and the birds; on the scarlet-barked willows and the delicate bareness of winter trees on the opposite side. Any one who had

come upon it now might have thought that the place
was under some spell. He would have seen the man
on the seat sit motionless, too, for a long time;
entranced rather than asleep: the scene had indeed
sunk down into his heart and 'Held it like a dream'.
There are times when man's consciousness seems
laid to rest in some great whole, of which he has
become a part. There are hours of which it can be
said, 'Thought was not: in enjoyment it expired.'
So it was now, and if anything stirred in the mind at
all, it was an echo of the words, 'And God saw that it
was good.'

Grey of Fallodon (1862-1933)
'The Charm of Birds

It is still winter and Thomas Hardy is not the only one braving
the cold.

THE DARKLING THRUSH

I leant upon a coppice gate
    When Frost was spectre-gray,
And Winter's dregs made desolate
    The weakening eye of day.
The tangled bine-stems scored the sky
    Like strings of broken lyres,
And all mankind that haunted nigh
    Had sought their household fires.

The land's sharp features seemed to be
    The Century's corpse outleant,
His crypt the cloudy canopy,
    The wind his death-lament.
The ancient pulse of germ and birth
    Was shrunken hard and dry,
And every spirit upon earth
    Seemed fervourless as I.

At once a voice arose among
    The bleak twigs overhead
In a full-hearted evensong
    Of joy illimited;

An aged thrush, frail, gaunt, and small,
   In blast-beruffled plume,
Had chosen thus to fling his soul
   Upon the growing gloom.

So little cause for carollings
   Of such ecstatic sound
Was written on terrestrial things
   Afar or nigh around,
That I could think there trembled through
   His happy good-night air
Some blessed Hope, whereof he knew
   And I was unaware.

                   Thomas Hardy (1840–1928)

St Francis of Assisi approached religion through joy in nature:
all creatures he called his brothers and sisters, and artists have
often portrayed him as preaching to the birds. After his death,
legends and anecdotes about his life were collected and published in the fourteenth century as *The Little Flowers of St
Francis*. He was so very human. Here are three of his little
flowers.

> Once when St Francis was about to eat with Brother
> Leo, he was greatly delighted to hear a nightingale
> singing. So he suggested to his companion that they
> also should sing praise to God alternately with the
> bird. While Leo was pleading that he was no singer,
> Francis lifted up his voice and, phrase by phrase,
> sang his duet with the nightingale. Thus they con-
> tinued from vespers to lauds, until the saint had to
> admit himself beaten by the bird. Thereupon the
> nightingale flew on to his hand, where he praised it
> to the skies and fed it. Then he gave it his blessing
> and it flew away.

> Brother Tebaldo once told us something that he
> himself had seen. When St Francis was preaching one
> day to the people of Trevi, a noisy and ungovernable
> ass went careering about the square, frightening
> people out of their wits. And when it became clear

that no one could catch it or restrain it, St Francis said to it, 'Brother ass, please be quiet and allow me to preach to the people.' When the donkey heard this it immediately bowed its head and, to everyone's astonishment, stood perfectly quiet. And the Blessed Francis, fearing that the people might take too much notice of this astonishing miracle, began saying funny things to make them laugh.

. Brother Masseo has said that he was present with the Blessed Francis when he preached to the birds. Rapt in devotion, Francis once found by the roadside a large flock of birds, to whom he turned aside to preach, as he had done before to another lot. But when the birds saw him approaching, they all flew away at the very sight of him. Then he came back and began to accuse himself most bitterly, saying, 'What effrontery you have, you impudent son of Peter Bernardone!'—and this because he had expected irrational creatures to obey him as if he, not God, were their Creator.

John R. H. Moorman: 'The New Fioretti'

Lord make me an instrument of Your peace
  Where there is hatred let me sow love,
  Where there is injury, pardon,
  Where there is doubt, faith,
  Where there is despair, hope,
  Where there is darkness, light,
  Where there is sadness, joy.
O Divine Master, grant that I may not so much seek to be consoled as to console; to be understood as to understand; to be loved as to love; for it is in giving that we receive; it is in pardoning that we are pardoned and it is in dying that we are born to eternal life.

Prayer of St Francis (1181?–1226)

William Blake's devoted wife is once supposed to have said: 'I have little of Mr Blake's company; he is always in Paradise.'

There are a lot of other husbands who might wish they got off so lightly.

How strange it is that people look at nature in such different ways. In Blake's words: 'As a man is, so he sees.'

> I know that This World is a World of Imagination and Vision. I see Every thing I paint In This World, but Every body does not see alike. To the Eyes of a Miser a Guinea is far more beautiful than the Sun, and a bag worn with the use of money has more beautiful proportions than a Vine filled with Grapes. The tree which moves some to tears of joy is in the Eyes of others only a Green thing which stands in the way. Some see Nature all Ridicule and Deformity . . . and some scarce see Nature at all. But to the Eyes of the Man of Imagination, Nature is Imagination itself. As a man is, so he sees. As the Eye is formed, such are its Powers. You certainly Mistake, when you say that the Visions of Fancy are not to be found in This World. To me This World is all One continued Vision of Fancy or Imagination, and I feel Flattered when I am told so.
>
> *William Blake (1757–1827): Letter to the*
> *Rev. Dr Trusler*

> The wolf also shall dwell with the lamb, and the leopard shall lie down with the kid; and the calf and the young lion and the fatling together; and a little child shall lead them.
>
> And the cow and the bear shall feed; their young ones shall lie down together; and the lion shall eat straw like the ox.
>
> And the sucking child shall play on the hole of the asp, and the weaned child shall put his hand on the cockatrice' den.
>
> They shall not hurt nor destroy in all my holy mountain: for the earth shall be full of the knowledge of the Lord, as the waters cover the sea.
>
> *Isaiah 11: 6–9*

I'm nuts about ducks.

DUCKS

I

From troubles of the world
I turn to ducks,
Beautiful comical things
Sleeping or curled
Their heads beneath white wings
By water cool,
Or finding curious things
To eat in various mucks
Beneath the pool,
Tails uppermost, or waddling
Sailor-like on the shores
Of ponds, or paddling
— Left! right!— with fanlike feet
Which are for steady oars
When they (white galleys) float
Each bird a boat
Rippling at will the sweet
Wide waterway . . .
When night is fallen you creep
Upstairs, but drakes and dillies
Nest with pale water-stars,
Moonbeams and shadow bars,
And water-lilies:
Fearful too much to sleep
Since they've no locks
To click against the teeth
Of weasel and fox.
And warm beneath
Are eggs of cloudy green
Whence hungry rats and lean
Would stealthily suck
New life, but for the mien,
The bold ferocious mien
Of the mother-duck.

II

Yes, ducks are valiant things
On nests of twigs and straws,

And ducks are soothy things
And lovely on the lake
When that the sunlight draws
Thereon their pictures dim
In colours cool.
And when beneath the pool
They dabble, and when they swim
And make their rippling rings,
O ducks are beautiful things!

But ducks are comical things:—
As comical as you.
Quack!
They waddle round, they do.
They eat all sorts of things,
And then they quack.
By barn and stable and stack
They wander at their will,
But if you go too near
They look at you through black
Small topaz-tinted eyes
And wish you ill.
Triangular and clear
They leave their curious track
In mud at the water's edge,
And there amid the sedge
And slime they gobble and peer
Saying 'Quack! Quack!'   *F. W. Harvey (1888–1957)*

With age I have become somewhat converted to cats. We have always had cats at home but only recently have I started to appreciate them fully. They are so perfectly self-contained and dignified. This is a honey of a poem.

MILK FOR THE CAT

When the tea is brought at five o'clock,
And all the neat curtains are drawn with care,
The little black cat with bright green eyes
Is suddenly purring there.

At first she pretends, having nothing to do,
She has come in merely to blink by the grate,

But, though tea may be late or the milk may be sour,
She is never late.

And presently her agate eyes
Take a soft large milky haze,
And her independent casual glance
Becomes a stiff, hard gaze.

Then she stamps her claw or lifts her ears,
Or twists her tail and begins to stir,
Till suddenly all her lithe body becomes
One breathing, trembling purr.

The children eat and wriggle and laugh;
The two old ladies stroke their silk:
But the cat is grown small and thin with desire,
Transformed to a creeping lust for milk.

The white saucer like some full moon descends
At last from the clouds of the table above;
She sighs and dreams and thrills and glows,
Transfigured with love.

She nestles over the shining rim,
Buries her chin in the creamy sea;
Her tail hangs loose; each drowsy paw
Is doubled under each bending knee.

A long, dim ecstasy holds her life;
Her world is an infinite shapeless white,
Till her tongue has curled the last holy drop,
Then she sinks back into the night.

Draws and dips her body to heap
Her sleepy nerves in the great arm-chair,
Lies defeated and buried deep
Three or four hours unconscious there.

Harold Monro (1879–193²

Another splendid cat poem was written by Sir Alexander Gray
I especially sympathise with the last two lines.

ON A CAT, AGEING

He blinks upon the hearth-rug,
And yawns in deep content,
Accepting all comforts
That Providence has sent.

Loud he purrs and louder,
In one glad hymn of praise
For all the night's adventures,
For quiet restful days.

Life will go on for ever,
With all that cat can wish,
Warmth and the glad procession
Of fish and milk and fish.

Only—the thought disturbs him—
He's noticed once or twice
The times are somehow breeding
A nimbler race of mice.

Alexander Gray (1882–1968)

What a perfect fishing mentor Izaak Walton must have been.
The scholar was fortunate indeed. In *The Compleat Angler*
Piscator (an angler) tries to convince Venator (a hunter) that
angling is a superior sport.

> *Piscator:* Look you, scholar, I have yet another. And
> now, having caught three brace of trouts, I will tell
> you a short tale as we walk towards our breakfast.
> A scholar, a preacher I should say, that was to preach
> to procure the approbation of a parish that he might
> be their lecturer, had got from his fellow-pupil the
> copy of a sermon that was first preached with great
> commendation by him that composed it; and though
> the borrower of it preached it, word by word, as it
> was at first, yet it was utterly disliked as it was
> preached by the second to his congregation; which
> the sermon borrower complained of to the lender of
> it; and thus was answered: 'I lent you, indeed, my
> fiddle, but not my fiddle-stick; for you are to know

that every one cannot make music with my words, which are fitted to my own mouth.' And so, my scholar, you are to know, that as the ill pronunciation or ill accenting of words in a sermon spoils it, so the ill carriage of your line, or not fishing even to a foot in a right place, makes you lose your labour: and you are to know, that though you have my fiddle, that is, my very rod and tacklings with which you see I catch fish, yet you have not my fiddle-stick, that is, you yet have not skill to know how to carry your hand and line, nor how to guide it to a right place; and this must be taught you; for you are to remember, I told you angling is an art, either by practice or a long observation, or both. But take this for a rule: when you fish for a trout with a worm, let your line have so much and not more lead than will fit the stream in which you fish; that is to say, more in a great troublesome stream than in a smaller that is quieter; as near as may be, so much as will sink the bait to the bottom, and keep it still in motion, and not more.

But now, let's say grace, and fall to breakfast. What say you, scholar, to the providence of an old angler? does not this meat taste well? and was not this place well chosen to eat it? for this sycamore-tree will shade us from the sun's heat.

Venator: All excellent good, and my stomach excellent good too.

Izaak Walton (1593–1683): 'The Compleat Angler'

Frances Cornford who died in 1960 was the grand-daughter of Charles Darwin. This poem is somewhat childish but remember feeling exactly the same about a puppy. The last line is inspired.

FÉRI'S DREAM

I had a little dog, and my dog was very small;
He licked me in the face, and he answered to my call,
Of all the treasures that were mine, I loved him best
   of all.

His nose was fresh as morning dew and blacker than
    the night;
I thought that it could even snuff the shadows and
    the light;
And his tail he held bravely like a banner in a fight.

His body covered thick with hair was very good to
    smell;
His little stomach underneath was pink as any shell;
And I loved him and honoured him, more than words
    can tell.

We ran out in the morning, both of us, to play,
Up and down across the fields for all the sunny day;
But he ran so swiftly—he ran right away.

I looked for him, I called for him, intreatingly. Alas,
The dandelions could not speak, though they had
    seen him pass,
And nowhere was his waving tail among the waving
    grass.

The sun sank low. I ran; I prayed: 'If God has not
    the power
To find him, let me die. I cannot live another hour.'
When suddenly I came upon a great yellow flower.

And all among its petals, such was Heaven's grace,
In that golden hour, in that golden place,
All among its petals, was his hairy face.

        Frances Cornford (1886–1960): from 'Féri Bekassy'

I love this too.

MAN AND DOG

Who's this—alone with stone and sky?
It's only my old dog and I—
It's only him; it's only me;
Alone with stone and grass and tree.

What share we most—we two together?
Smells, and awareness of the weather.

What is it makes us more than dust?
My trust in him; in me his trust.

Here's anyhow one decent thing
That life to man and dog can bring;
One decent thing, remultiplied
Till earth's last dog and man have died.

Siegfried Sassoon (1886–1933)

Richard Jefferies again.

THE HAPPINESS OF ANIMALS

Just outside the trench, almost within reach, there
lies a small white something, half hidden by the
grass. It is the skull of a hare, bleached by the winds
and the dew and the heat of the summer sun. The
skeleton has disappeared, nothing but the bony casing
of the head remains, with its dim suggestiveness of
life, polished and smooth from the friction of the
elements. Holding it in the hand the shadow falls
into and darkens the cavities once filled by the wist-
ful eyes which whilom glanced down from the
summit here upon the sweet clover fields beneath.

The joy in life of these animals—indeed, of almost
all animals and birds in freedom—is very great.
You may see it in every motion—in the lissom bound
of the hare, the playful leap of the rabbit, the song
that the lark and the finch must sing; the soft
loving coo of the dove in the hawthorn; the blackbird ruffling out his feathers on a rail. The sense of
living—the consciousness of seeing and feeling—is
manifestly intense in them all, and is in itself an
exquisite pleasure.

Richard Jefferies (1848–1887):
'Wild Life in a Southern County'

All the remoteness and power of the eagle is in this short
poem by Tennyson.

THE EAGLE

He clasps the crag with crooked hands;
Close to the sun in lonely lands,
Ring'd with the azure world, he stands.

The wrinkled sea beneath him crawls;
He watches from his mountain walls,
And like a thunderbolt he falls.

Alfred Tennyson (1809–1892)

J. A. Baker's obsession is peregrines. In his extraordinary first book he describes the ten-year-long pursuit of a magnificent bird of prey whose numbers have sadly decreased in England.

I scanned the sky constantly to see if a hawk was soaring, scrutinised every tree and bush, searched the apparently empty sky through every arc. That is how the hawk finds his prey and eludes his enemies, and that is the only way one can hope to find him and share his hunting. Binoculars, and a hawk-like vigilance, reduce the disadvantage of myopic human vision.

At last, yet one more of all the distant pigeon-like birds, that till then had always proved to be pigeons, was suddenly the peregrine. He flew over South Wood, and soared in the warm air rising from open spaces sheltered by encircling trees. Crisp and golden in the sunlight, he swam up through the warm air with muscular undulations of his wings, like the waving flicker of a fish's fins. He drifted on the surface, a tiny silver flake on the blue burnish of the sky. His wings tightened and bent back, and he slid away to the east, a dark blade cutting slowly through blue ice. Moving down through sunlight, he changed colour like an autumn leaf, passing from shining gold to pallid yellow, turning from tawny to brown, suddenly flicking out black against the skyline.

White fire smouldered in the south as the sun glared lower. Two jackdaws flew high above. One dived, went into a spin, looped the loop, and fell towards earth as though it had been shot, a tossing bag of bones and feathers. It was playing at being dead. When a foot from the ground, it spread its wings and dropped lightly down, superbly nonchalant.

Following the restless plover, I crossed the brook and found the falcon peregrine in a hedge to the west. I stalked her, but she moved from tree to tree along the hedge, keeping up against the sun, where she could see me clearly while I was dazzled. When the hedge ended, she flew to a tree by the brook. She seemed sleepy and lethargic and did not move her head much. Her eyes had a brown ceramic glaze. They watched my eyes intently. I turned away for a moment. She flew at once. I looked back quickly, but she had gone. Hawks are reluctant to fly while they are being watched. They wait till the strange bondage of the eyes is broken.

Gulls flew slowly over to the east, their wings transparent in the brilliant light. At three o'clock the falcon cricled among them, and began to soar. It was high tide at the estuary. Waders would be swirling up and sinking down above the creeks and saltings like blood pounding in a caged heart. I knew the peregrine would see them, would see the thousands of gulls moving in towards the brimming water, and I thought she would follow them eastward. Without waiting longer, I cycled as fast as I could across to a small hill, six miles away, that overlooks the estuary. Twice I stopped and searched for the falcon and found her circling high above the wooded ridge, drifting east as I had hoped. By the time I reached the hill she had passed over and down.

In the small lens of light that the telescope cored out from three miles of sunlit intervening air, I saw the shining water of the estuary darken and seethe with birds and the sharp hook of the falcon rising and falling in a long crenellation of stoops. Then the dark water lifted to brightness again, and all was still.

J. A. Baker (1926–): 'The Peregrine'

Francis Thompson was greatly influenced by Wordsworth, Keats and Shelley. Here he speculates on the heart of Nature. I like his thought: 'She is God's daughter, who stretches her hand only to her Father's friends.'

What is this heart of Nature, if it exist at all? Is it, according to the conventional doctrine derived from Wordsworth and Shelley, a heart of love, according with the heart of man, and stealing out to him through a thousand avenues of mute sympathy? No; in this sense . . . Nature has no heart.

I sit now, alone and melancholy, with that melancholy which comes to all of us when the waters of sad knowledge have left their ineffaceable delta in the soul. As I write, a calm, faint-tinted evening sky sinks like a nestward bird to its sleep. At a little distance is a dark wall of fir-wood; while close at hand a small group of larches rise like funeral plumes against that tranquil sky, and seem to say 'Night cometh'. They alone are in harmony with me. All else speaks to me of a beautiful, peaceful world in which I have no part. And did I go up to yonder hill, and behold at my feet the spacious amphitheatre of hill-girt wood and mead, overhead the mighty aerial velarium, I should feel that my human sadness was a higher and deeper and wider thing than all. O Titan Nature! a petty race, which has dwarfed its spirit in dwellings, and bounded it in selfish shallows of art, may find you too vast, may shrink from you into its earths; but though you be a very large thing, and my heart a very little thing, yet Titan as you are, my heart is too great for you. . . . Absolute Nature lives not in our life, nor yet is lifeless, but lives in the life of God; and in so far, and so far merely, as man himself lives in that life, does he come into sympathy with Nature, and Nature with him. She is God's daughter, who stretches her hand only to her Father's friends. Not Shelley, not Wordsworth himself, ever drew so close to the heart of Nature as did the Seraph of Assisi, who was close to the Heart of God.

Francis Thompson (1859–1907): 'Works', vol. III

PIED BEAUTY

Glory be to God for dappled things—
    For skies of couple-colour as a brinded cow;
      For rose-moles all in stipple upon trout that
        swim;
Fresh-firecoal chestnut-falls; finches' wings;
    Landscape-plotted and pieced—fold, fallow, and
      plough;
      And áll trádes, their gear and tackle and trim.

All things counter, original, spare, strange;
    Whatever is fickle, freckled (who knows how?)
      With swift, slow; sweet, sour; adazzle, dim;
He fathers-forth whose beauty is past change:
                   Praise him.
           Gerard Manley Hopkins (1844–188

SECTION THREE

SECTION THREE

LOVE AND FRIENDSHIP

PRELUDE

Love bade me welcome: yet my soul drew back,
   Guiltie of dust and sinne.
But quick-ey'd Love, observing me grow slack
   From my first entrance in,
Drew nearer to me, sweetly questioning,
   If I lack'd any thing.

A guest, I answer'd, worthy to be here:
   Love said, You shall be he.
I the unkinde, ungratefull? Ah my deare,
   I cannot look on thee.
Love took my hand, and smiling did reply,
   Who made the eyes but I?

> Truth Lord, but I have marr'd them: let my shame
>   Go where it doth deserve.
> And know you not, sayes Love, who bore the blame?
>   My deare, then I will serve.
> You must sit down, sayes Love, and taste my meat:
>   So I did sit and eat.
>
> *George Herbert* (1593-1633): *'The Temple'*

'Love' must be one of the most overworked and misused words in the English language.

Kierkegaard, the nineteenth-century Danish philosopher, gives here a reminder of its true meaning. T. H. Croxall said of him: 'If we took Kierkegaard seriously and ask ourselves some of the exacting questions he puts to us, then we might be better equipped to face the invading and expanding tides of materialism and despair.'

> What is it that makes a man great, admired by his fellows, acceptable in the sight of God? What is it that makes a man strong, stronger than the whole world, what is it that makes him weak, weaker than a child? What is it that makes a man immovable, more immovable than the rock, what is it that makes him soft, softer than wax? It is love! What is it that is older than everything else? It is love! What is it that outlives everything else? It is love. What is it that cannot be taken, but itself takes everything? It is love. What is it that cannot be given, but itself gives everything? It is love. What is it that endures when all else disappoints? It is love. What is it that comforts when all comfort fails? It is love. What is it that persists when all else changes? It is love. What is it that remains when the imperfect is abolished? It is love. What is it that bears witness when prophecy is silent? It is love. What is it that does not end when vision ceases? It is love. What is it that explains when the dark saying is ended? It is love. What is it that bestows a blessing on the abundance of the gift? It is love. What is it that gives emphasis to the speech of angels? It is love. What is it that transforms the widow's mite into an abundance? It is

love. What is it that turns the words of the simple
man into wisdom? It is love. What is it that never
changes when all else changes? It is love; and only
that is love which never becomes anything else.
      Søren Kierkegaard (1813–1855): 'Edifying Discourses'

And we must surely listen to what one of the greatest thinkers
of all time had to say about it.

Love seems to me, O Phaedrus, a divinity the most
beautiful and the best of all, and the author to all
others of the excellencies with which his own nature
is endowed. Nor can I restrain the poetic enthusiasm
which takes possession of my discourse, and bids me
declare that Love is the divinity who creates peace
among men, and calm upon the sea, the windless
silence of storms, repose and sleep in sadness. Love
divests us of all alienation from each other, and
fills our vacant hearts with overflowing sympathy; he
gathers us together in such social meetings as we now
delight to celebrate, our guardian and our guide in
dances, and sacrifices, and feasts. Yes, Love, who
showers benignity upon the world, and before whose
presence all harsh passions flee and perish; the
author of all soft affections; the destroyer of all un-
gentle thoughts; merciful, mild; the object of the
admiration of the wise, and the delight of gods;
possessed by the fortunate, and desired by the unhappy, therefore unhappy because they possess him
not; the father of grace, and delicacy, and gentleness, and delight, and persuasion, and desire; the
cherisher of all that is good, the abolisher of evil;
our most excellent pilot, defence, saviour and
guardian in labour and in fear, in desire and in
reason; the ornament and governor of all things
human and divine; the best, the loveliest; in whose
footsteps everyone ought to follow, celebrating him
excellently in song, and bearing each his part in that
divinest harmony which Love sings to all things
which live and are, soothing the troubled minds of
Gods and men.
      The Banquet from 'Five Dialogues of Plato' (?427–347? B.C.)
                                     'On Poetic Inspiration'

... My neighbour, or my servant, or my child, has
done me an injury, and it is just that he should
suffer an injury in return. Such is the doctrine which
Jesus Christ summoned his whole resources of
persuasion to oppose. 'Love your enemy; bless those
that curse you': such, he says, is the practice of God,
and such must ye imitate if ye would be the children of
God.

*Shelley: copied from Mr Bowyer Nichols' quotation
in 'Words and Days', 1895, for Christmas Day*

William Blake in one of his friskier moods.

THE ANGEL AND THE THIEF

I asked a Thief to steal me a peach
He turned up his eyes.
I asked a lithe lady to lie her down
'Holy and Meek' she cries.

As soon as I went an Angel came.
He winked at the Thief and smiled at the dame.

And without one word spoke
Had a peach from the tree
And 'twixt earnest and jest
Enjoyed the lady.

William Blake (1757–1827)

Words of great wisdom now from Frederick Max Müller, son
of the German poet Wilhelm Müller, who became a natural-
ised British subject in 1846 and settled in Oxford to become a
professor of comparative philology.

We must not forget that if earthly love has in the
vulgar mind been often degraded into mere animal
passion, it still remains in its purest sense the highest
mystery of our existence, the most perfect blessing
and delight on earth, and at the same time the
truest pledge of our more than human nature.

Would not the carrying out of one single commandment of Christ, 'Love one another', change the whole aspect of the world, and sweep away prisons and workhouses, and envying and strife, and all the strongholds of the devil? Two thousand years have nearly passed, and people have not yet understood that one single command of Christ, 'Love one another'!

If we do a thing because we think it is our duty, we generally fail; that is the old law which makes slaves of us. The real spring of our life, and of our work in life, must be love—true, deep love—not love of this or that person, or for this or that reason, but deep human love, devotion of soul to soul, love of God realised where alone it can be—in love of those whom He loves. Everything else is weak, passes away; that love alone supports us, makes life tolerable, binds the present together with the past and future, and is, we may trust, imperishable.

How selfish we are even in our love! Here we live for a short season, and we know we must part sooner or later. We wish to go first, and to leave those whom we love behind us, and we sorrow because they went first and left us behind. As soon as one looks beyond this life, it seems so short; yet there was a time when it seemed endless.

The past is ours, and there we have all who loved us, and whom we love as much as ever, ay, more than ever.

Max Müller (1823–1900): 'Thought on Life and Religion'

TRUE LOVE

My true love hath my heart and I have his,
　By just exchange one for another given;
I hold his dear, and mine he cannot miss,
　There never was a better bargain driven.
　My true love hath my heart and I have his.

His heart in me keeps him and me in one,
    My heart in him his thoughts and senses guides;
He loves my heart, for once it was his own,
    I cherish his, because in me it bides.
    My true love hath my heart and I have his.
                              Sir Philip Sidney (1554–1586)

H. G. Wells was not one of our great romantic novelists ye
in *Ann Veronica* his heroine, having been involved with the
women's suffrage movement, finds she is nevertheless sur-
prisingly susceptible to the opposite sex.

Then one day a little thing happened that clothed
itself in significance.

She had been working upon a ribbon of microtome
sections of the developing salamander, and he came
to see what she had made of them. She stood up and
he sat down at the microscope, and for a time he was
busy scrutinizing one section after another. She
looked down at him and saw that the sunlight was
gleaming from his cheeks, and that all over his
cheeks was a fine golden down of delicate hairs. And
at the sight something leapt within her. Something
changed for her.

She became aware of his presence as she had never
been aware of any human being in her life before.
She became aware of the modelling of his ear, of the
muscles of his neck and the textures of the hair that
came off his brow, the soft minute curve of eyelid
that she could just see beyond his brow; she per-
ceived all these familiar objects as though they were
acutely beautiful things. They *were*, she realized,
acutely beautiful things. Her senses followed the
shoulders under his coat, down to where his flexible,
sensitive-looking hand rested lightly on the table.
She felt him as something solid and strong and trust-
worthy beyond measure. The perception of him
flooded her being.

He got up. 'Here's something rather good,' he said,
and with a start and an effort she took his place at
the microscope, while he stood beside her and almost
leaning over her.

She found she was trembling at his nearness and full of a thrilling dread that he might touch her. She pulled herself together and put her eye to the eye-piece.

'You see the pointer?' he asked.

'I see the pointer,' she said.

'It's like this,' he said, and dragged a stool beside her and sat down with his elbow four inches from hers and made a sketch. Then he got up and left her.

She had a feeling at his departure as of an immense cavity, of something enormously gone; she could not tell whether it was infinite regret or infinite relief. . . .

But now Ann Veronica knew what was the matter with her.

H. G. Wells (1866–1946): 'Ann Veronica'

I'm sure I am not the only man who has felt as Robert Graves did when he wrote these lines.

A SLICE OF WEDDING CAKE

Why have such scores of lovely, gifted girls
    Married impossible men?
Simple self-sacrifice may be ruled out,
    And missionary endeavour, nine times out of ten.

Repeat 'impossible men': not merely rustic,
    Foul-tempered or depraved
(Dramatic foils chosen to show the world
    How well women behave, and always have
      behaved).

Impossible men: idle, illiterate,
    Self-pitying, dirty, sly,
For whose appearance even in City parks
    Excuses must be made to casual passers-by.

Has God's supply of tolerable husbands
    Fallen, in fact, so low?

> Or do I always over-value woman
>   At the expense of man?
>   Do I?
>   It might be so.
>   *Robert Graves (1895–)*

So, no problem in drinking to this toast:

> Here's to the maiden of bashful fifteen;
>   Here's to the widow of fifty;
> Here's to the flaunting, extravagant quean;
>   And here's to the housewife that's thrifty.
>   Let the toast pass,—
>   Drink to the lass,
> I'll warrant she'll prove an excuse for the glass.
>
> Here's to the charmer
>   Whose dimples we prize;
> Now to the maid who has
>   none, sir;
> Here's to the girl with a pair
>   of blue eyes,
> And here's to the nymph with but one, sir.
>   *Richard Brinsley Sheridan (1751–1816):*
>   *'The School for Scandal'*

And Sheridan pays here the perfect compliment:

> Won't you come into the garden? I would like my
> roses to see you.
>   *To a young lady. Attributed in 'The Perfect Hostess'*

This is surely one of the greatest love poems ever written.

A RED RED ROSE

> O my Luve's like a red, red rose,
>   That's newly sprung in June;
> O my Luve's like the melodie
>   That's sweetly play'd in tune.—

As fair art thou, my bonie lass,
  So deep in luve am I;
And I will love thee still, my Dear,
  Till a' the seas gang dry.—

Till a' the seas gang dry, my Dear,
  And the rocks melt wi' the sun:
I will love thee still, my Dear,
  While the sands o' life shall run.—

And fare thee weel, my only Luve!
  And fare thee weel, a while!
And I will come again, my Luve,
  Tho' it were ten thousand mile!

Robert Burns (1759–96)

SHE WALKS IN BEAUTY

She walks in beauty, like the night
  Of cloudless climes and starry skies;
And all that's best of dark and bright
  Meet in her aspect and her eyes:
Thus mellowed to that tender light
  Which heaven to gaudy day denies.

One shade the more, one ray the less,
  Had half impaired the nameless grace
Which waves in every raven tress,
  Or softly lightens o'er her face;
Where thoughts serenely sweet express
  How pure, how dear their dwelling-place.

And on that cheek and o'er that brow
  So soft, so calm, yet eloquent,
The smiles that win, the tints that glow
  But tell of days in goodness spent,
A mind at peace with all below,
  A heart whose love is innocent!

George Gordon Byron (1788–1824)

Turgenev was the most European of the great Russian writers.
Here, in his novel *Home of the Gentry*, his hero Lavretsky,

recently returned from Western Europe, sees Liza a young local girl in church.

> The next day Lavretsky went to church. Liza was already there when he arrived. She noticed him although she did not turn towards him. She prayed with great devotion; her eyes radiated a quiet reverence, with quiet reverence she bowed and raised her head. He felt that she was praying for him as well, and he felt wonderfully uplifted in his soul. It was a feeling both happy and a little conscience-stricken. The people standing there in their Sunday best, the familiar faces, the harmonious singing, the smell of incense, the long oblique rays of sunlight from the windows, the very darkness of the walls and vaulted ceiling—everything spoke directly to his heart. It was a long time since he had been in a church, a long time since he had addressed himself to God; he uttered no words of prayer now—and he did not pray even wordlessly—but if only for an instant, if not with his body, then with all his being, he cast himself down and bowed in humility to the ground. He was reminded how in his childhood, on each visit to the church, he would pray until such time as he felt upon his brow the touch of something sent to refresh him; that, he used to think, was his guardian angel taking him into his keeping and setting upon him the seal of grace. He glanced at Liza. . . . 'You've brought me here,' he thought, 'stretch out your hand and touch me, touch my soul.' She still prayed with the same quiet reverence; her face seemed to him radiant with joy, and again he was uplifted, and he begged peace for another person's soul and forgiveness for his own. . . .
> They met at the entrance to the church; she greeted him with a fond and cheerful gravity. The sun shone brightly on the young grass in front of the church and the colourful dresses and headwear of the women; the bells of neighbouring churches boomed high above; sparrows chattered on the fences; Lavretsky stood smiling with uncovered head; a light breeze flicked up his hair and the ends of the

ribbons of Liza's hat. He helped Liza, and Lenochka who was accompanying her, into the carriage, distributed all the money he had with him to the beggars and went quietly home.

Ivan Turgenev (1818–1883): 'Home of the Gentry'

TO MY WIFE

I know you, wife;
Know you as life crumples your clothes,
Weaves at your face, and passes.
In some part of the milkman's world
You are a smile. Shopkeepers and friends
Gleam in its separate lights and think
They understand. All that our children know
Of you warms them like their blankets,
Tucked by your everlasting hands.
But I, for whom these things
Mean new expenses and the loss of you,
Know you as a bird can know its wings,
A salmon its return.
You have left sounds in every room
Protecting me from loneliness, and if
One day I take a car
And find a land to plunder where your face
Does not arrest me like a fundamental law,
Necessity will teach me
That your name is Love.

Peter Firth

A WIFE TO A HUSBAND

How do I love thee? Let me count the ways.
I love thee to the depth and breadth and height
My soul can reach, when feeling out of sight
For the end of Being and ideal Grace.
I love thee to the level of everyday's
Most quiet need, by sun and candlelight.
I love thee freely, as men strive for Right;
I love thee purely, as they turn from Praise.
I love thee with the passion put to use
In my old griefs, and with my childhood's faith.

I love thee with a love I seemed to lose
With my lost saints,—I love thee with the breath,
Smiles, tears, of all my life!—and, if God choose,
I shall but love thee better after death.

Elizabeth Barrett Browning (1806–1861)
'Sonnets from the Portuguese

Love takes many forms: miners often love the beauty o
flowers. D. H. Lawrence, who was himself the son of a
Nottinghamshire miner, writes of his boyhood and of the
colliers he knew so well. It's powerfully evocative even if he
wasn't quite fair to their wives.

We lived in the Breach, in a corner house. A field-
path came down under a great hawthorn hedge. On
the other side was the brook, with the old sheep-
bridge going over into the meadows. The hawthorn
hedge by the brook had grown tall as tall trees,
and we used to bathe from there in the dipping
hole, where the sheep were dipped, just near the
fall from the old mill-dam, where the water rushed.
The mill only ceased grinding the local corn when
I was a child. And my father, who always worked in
Brinsley pit, and who always got up at five o'clock,
if not at four, would set off in the dawn across the
fields at Coney Grey, and hunt for mushrooms in
the long grass, or perhaps pick up a skulking rabbit,
which he would bring home at evening inside the
lining of his pit-coat.

So that the life was a curious cross between in-
dustrialism and the old agricultural England of
Shakespeare and Milton and Fielding and George
Eliot. The dialect was broad Derbyshire, and always
'thee' and 'thou'. The people lived almost entirely
by instinct, men of my father's age could not really
read. And the pit did not mechanize men. On the
contrary. Under the butty system, the miners worked
underground as a sort of intimate community, they
knew each other practically naked, and with curious
close intimacy, and the darkness and the underground remoteness of the pit 'stall', and the con-

tinual presence of danger, made the physical, instinctive, and intuitional contact almost as close as touch, very real and very powerful. This physical awareness and intimate *togetherness* was at its strongest down pit. When the men came up into the light, they blinked. They had, in a measure, to change their flow. Nevertheless, they brought with them above ground the curious dark intimacy of the mine, the naked sort of contact, and if I think of my childhood, it is always as if there was a lustrous sort of inner darkness, like the gloss of coal, in which we moved and had our real being. My father loved the pit. He was hurt badly, more than once, but he would never stay away. He loved the contact, the intimacy, as men in the war loved the intense male comradeship of the dark days. They did not know what they had lost till they lost it. And I think it is the same with the young colliers of today.

Now the colliers had also an instinct of beauty. The colliers' wives had not. The colliers were deeply alive, instinctively. But they had no daytime ambition, and no daytime intellect. They avoided, really, the rational aspect of life. They preferred to take life instinctively and intuitively. They didn't even care very profoundly about wages. It was the women, naturally, who nagged on this score. There was a big discrepancy, when I was a boy, between the collier who saw, at the best, only a brief few hours of daylight—often no daylight at all during the winter weeks—and the collier's wife, who had all the day to herself when the man was down pit.

The great fallacy is, to pity the man. He didn't dream of pitying himself, till agitators and sentimentalists taught him to. He was happy: or more than happy, he was fulfilled. Or he was fulfilled on the receptive side, not on the expressive. The collier went to the pub and drank in order to continue his intimacy with his mates. They talked endlessly, but it was rather of wonders and marvels, even in politics, than of facts. It was hard facts, in the shape of wife, money, and nagging home necessities, which they fled away from, out of the house to the pub, and out of the house to the pit.

The collier fled out of the house as soon as he could, away from the nagging materialism of the woman. With the women it was always: This is broken, now you've got to mend it! or else: We want this, that and the other, and where is the money coming from? The collier didn't know and didn't care very deeply—his life was otherwise. So he escaped. He roved the countryside with his dog, prowling for a rabbit, for nests, for mushrooms, anything. He loved the countryside, just the indiscriminating feel of it. Or he loved just to sit on his heels and watch—anything or nothing. He was not intellectually interested. Life for him did not consist in facts, but in a flow. Very often he loved his garden. And very often he had a genuine love of the beauty of flowers. I have known it often and often, in colliers.

> D. H. Lawrence (1885–1930): 'Phoenix'

TWO LETTERS

The first, from a country boy to his girl, was picked up on the beach at Sidmouth in 1887 by William de Morgan.

'Dear Marey, dear Marey, I hant got no partcler news to tell ye at present but my sister that marryd have got such a nice littel babey, and I wish how as that we had got such a little dear too. Dearest Mary, I shall not be happy until then. Dearest Mary pure and holy meek and loly lovely Rose of Sharon. Sometimes I do begin to despare as I am afraid our knot will never be tied, but my Master have promised I how as that when I git ye he will put ye in the Dairy yard to feed the Piggs and give ye atin pense a week. . . . I be coming over tomorrow to buy the ring and you must come to the stashun to meet me and bring a pese of string with you the size of your finger. . . . Father is going to give us a bedstead and Granny a 5 lb note to buy such as washing stand fire irons mousetrap and Sope, and we must wayte till we can buy carpeting and glass, crockery-ware and chiny. . . . And Father is going to get us a Rooseter for our Weding Brakefast. Dearest Mary pure and holey

meek and loly lovely Rose of Sharon. So no more
at present from your future husband William
Taylor.'

And this was written in the Thirties by a girl in a hospital
ward in London, on the day before her death.

'Dear Alf, I seen you last night in my dream. O my
dear I cried waking up. What a silly girl you been
and got! The pain is bad this morning but I laugh
at the sollum looks of the sisters and the sawbones.
I can see they think I am booked but they dont know
what has befallen between you and me. How could
I die and leave my dear. I spill my medecine this
morning thinking of my dear. Hoping this finds you
well no more now yours truly Liz.'

A tribute to the staunchest of wives. Forty years is a long time.

'Tis forty years now since we were wed:
We are ailing an' grey needs not be said:
But Willie's eye is as blue an' soft
As the day when he wooed me in father's croft.

Yet changed am I in body an' mind,
For Willie to me has ne'er been kind:
Merrily drinking an' singing with the men
He 'ud come home late six nights o' the se'n.

An' since the children be grown an' gone
He 'as shunned the house an' left me lone:
An' less an' less he brings me in
Of the little now he has strength to win.

The roof lets through the wind an' the wet,
An' master won't mend it with us in's debt:
An' all looks every day more worn,
An' the best of my gowns be shabby an' torn.

No wonder if words hav' a-grown to blows;
That matters not while nobody knows:

For love him I shall to the end of life,
An' be, as I swore, his own true wife.

An' when I am gone, he'll turn, an' see
His folly an' wrong, an' be sorry for me:
An' come to me there in the land o' bliss
To give me the love I looked for in this.

Robert Bridges (1884–1930):
'Shorter Poems', Bk. V. 18

A tender, ecstatic love poem now from that contemporary American poet with the eccentric style, e.e. cummings.

the great advantage of being alive
(instead of undying) is not so much
that mind no more can disprove than prove
what heart may feel and soul may touch
—the great (my darling) happens to be
that love are in we, that love are in we

and here is a secret they never will share
for whom create is less than have
or one times one than when times where—
that we are in love, that love are in love:
with us they've nothing times nothing to do
(for love are in we am in i are in you)

This world (as timorous itsters all
to call their cowardice quite agree)
shall never discover our touch and feel
—for love are in we are in love are in we;
for you are and i am and we are (above
and under all possible worlds) in love

a billion brains may coax undeath
from fancied fact and spaceful time—
no heart can leap, no soul can breathe
but by the sizeless truth of a dream
whose sleep is the sky and the earth and the sea.
For love are in you am in i are in we

e. e. cummings (1894–1962)

Family life today is taking some hard knocks. Telly doesn't

help much, especially when it is a substitute for family small-talk. It seems to me that the qualities Benjamin Jowett wrote of in the last century are as desirable as ever they were. The great thing is to keep communication going in the family.

> The family, like the home in which they live, needs to be kept in repair, lest some little rift in the walls should appear and let in the wind and rain. The happiness of a family depends very much on attention to little things. Order, comfort, regularity, cheerfulness, good taste, pleasant conversation—these are the ornaments of daily life, deprived of which it degenerates into a wearisome routine. There must be light in the dwelling, and brightness and pure spirits and cheerful smiles. Home is not usually the place of toil, but the place to which we return and rest from our labours; in which parents and children meet together and pass a joyful and careless hour. To have nothing to say to others at such times, in any rank of life, is a very unfortunate temper of mind, and may perhaps be regarded as a serious fault; at any rate, it makes a house vacant and joyless, and persons who are afflicted by this distemper should remember seriously that if it is not cured in time it will pursue them through life. It is one of the lesser troubles of the family; and there is yet another trouble—members of a family often misunderstand one another's characters. They are sensitive or shy or retired; or they have some fanciful sorrow which they cannot communicate to others; or something which was said to them has produced too deep an impression on their minds. In their own family they are like strangers; the in-experience of youth exaggerates this trial, and they have no one to whom they can turn for advice or help. This is the time for sympathy—the sympathy of a brother or sister, or father or mother—which unlocks the hidden sorrow, and purges away the perilous stuff which was depressing the mind and injuring the character. Sympathy, too, is the noblest exercise; of it is the Spirit of God working together with our spirit; it is warmth as well as light, putting

into us a new heart, and taking away the stony heart which is dead to its natural surroundings.

Benjamin Jowett (1817–1893): 'Selected Passages from the Theological Writings.' Ed. Lewis Campbell

The love-bond between mother and daughter. Colette, the popular French novelist of 'Claudine' fame, writes a tribute to her mother and first quotes one of her letters.

'Monsieur,
   You ask me to come and spend a week with you, which means I would be near my daughter, whom I adore. You who live with her, well know how rarely I see her, how much her presence delights me, and I am touched that you should ask me to come and see her. All the same I am not going to accept your kind invitation, for the time being at any rate. The reason is that my pink cactus is probably going to flower. It is a very rare plant I've been given, and I'm told that in our climate it flowers only once every four years. Now, I am already a very old woman; and if I went away when my pink cactus was going to flower, I am certain I shouldn't see it flower again.'

This note, signed, *Sidonie Colette, née Landoy*, was written by my mother to one of my husbands, the second. A year later she died, at the age of seventy-seven.

Whenever I feel myself inferior to everything about me, threatened by my own mediocrity, frightened by the discovery that a muscle has lost its strength, a desire its power, or a pain the keen edge of its bite, I can still hold up my head and say to myself: I am the daughter of the woman who wrote that letter— that letter and so many more that I have kept. This one tells me in ten lines that at seventy-six she was planning journeys and undertaking them, but that waiting for the bursting into bloom of a tropical flower, held everything up and silenced even her heart, made for love.

Colette (1873–1954): 'La Naissance du Jour'

94

And between father and son.

TO HIS SON, VINCENT CORBET, ON HIS BIRTH-DAY, NOVEMBER 10, 1630, BEING THEN THREE YEARS OLD

What I shall leave thee none can tell,
But all shall say I wish thee well;
I wish thee, Vin, before all wealth,
Both bodily and ghostly health:
Not too much wealth, nor wit, come to thee,
So much of either may undoe thee.
I wish thee learning, not for show,
Enough for to instruct, and know;
Not such as Gentlemen require,
To prate at Table, or at Fire.
I wish thee all thy mother's graces,
Thy father's fortunes, and his places,
I wish thee friends, and one at Court,
Not to build on, but support;
To keep thee, not in doing many
Oppressions, but from suffering any.
I wish thee peace in all thy ways,
Nor lazy nor contentious days;
And when thy soul and body part,
As innocent as now thou art.

Richard Corbet

This love has no need of words.

THE MEETING

As I went up and he came down, my little six-year
  boy,
Upon the stairs we met and kissed, I and my tender
  Joy.
O fond and true, as lovers do, we kissed and clasped
  and parted;
And I went up and he went down, refreshed and
  happy-hearted.

What need was there for any words, his face against
  my face?

95

And in the silence heart to heart spoke for a little
    space
Of tender things and thoughts on wings and secrets
    none discovers;
And I went up and he went down, a pair of happy
    lovers.

His clinging arms about my neck, what need was
    there for words?
O little heart that beat so fast like any fluttering
    bird's!
'I love,' his silence said, 'I love,' my silence answered
    duly;
And I went up and he went down comforted wonder-
    fully.

                 Katharine Tynan (1861–1931

Polonius, the garrulous old courtier, talks good sense here to
his son Laertes.

Polonius: Give thy thoughts no tongue
Nor any unproportioned thought his act.
Be thou familiar, but by no means vulgar.
The friends thou hast, and their adoption tried,
Grapple them to thy soul with hoops of steel;
But do not dull thy palm with entertainment
Of each new-hatched, unfledged comrade. Beware
Of entrance to a quarrel; but being in,
Bear't, that th'opposed may beware of thee.
Give every man thine ear, but few thy voice;
Take each man's censure, but reserve thy judgement.
Costly thy habit as thy purse can buy,
But not expressed in fancy; rich, not gaudy;
For the apparel oft proclaims the man . . .
Neither a borrower, nor a lender be,
For loan oft loses both itself and friend,
And borrowing dulls the edge of husbandry.
This above all: to thine own self be true,
And it must follow, as the night the day,
Thou canst not then be false to any man.
           William Shakespeare (1564–1616): 'Hamlet

A deeply moving poem now by Emily Brontë. She had a great affinity with her brother Branwell, who was a clerk on the Leeds and Manchester railway until he was sacked for negligence. Later, he took to opium and died of consumption. Nothing ever changed her love for him. It was ironical that she herself caught a severe cold at his funeral in 1848 and died a few months later.

REMEMBRANCE

Cold in the earth—and the deep snow piled above
    thee,
Far, far removed, cold in the dreary grave!
Have I forgot, my only Love, to love thee,
Severed at last by Time's all-severing wave?

Now, when alone, do my thoughts no longer hover
Over the mountains, on that northern shore,
Resting their wings where heath and fern-leaves
    cover
Thy noble heart for ever, ever more?

Cold in the earth—and fifteen wild Decembers
From those brown hills have melted into spring—
Faithful indeed is the spirit that remembers
After such years of change and suffering!

Sweet Love of youth, forgive if I forget thee
While the world's tide is bearing me along:
Other desires and other hopes beset me,
Hopes which obscure, but cannot do thee wrong!

No later light has lightened up my heaven;
No second morn has ever shone for me:
All my life's bliss from thy dear life was given—
All my life's bliss is in the grave with thee.

But, when the days of golden dreams had perished,
And even Despair was powerless to destroy,
Then did I learn how existence could be cherished,
Strengthened, and fed without the aid of joy;

Then did I check the tears of useless passion,
Weaned my young soul from yearning after thine;
Sternly denied its burning wish to hasten
Down to that tomb already more than mine!

And, even yet, I dare not let it languish,
Dare not indulge in Memory's rapturous pain;
Once drinking deep of that divinest anguish,
How could I seek the empty world again?

Emily Brontë (1818-1848)

Love and friendship between brothers: John Keats, aged twenty-three, writes to his brother George.

Sometimes I fancy an immense separation, and sometimes, as at present, a direct communication of Spirit with you. That will be one of the grandeurs of immortality—There will be no space and consequently the only commerce between spirits will be by their intelligence of each other—when they will completely understand each other—while we in the world merely comprehend each other in different degrees—the higher the degree of good so higher is our Love and friendship. . . . The reason why I do not feel at the present moment so far from you is that I remember your Ways and Manners and actions; I know your manner of thinking, your manner of feeling; I know what shape your joy or your sorrow would take; I know the manner of your walking, standing, sauntering, sitting down, laughing, punning, and every action so truly that you seem near to me. You will remember me in the same manner—and the more when I tell you that I shall read a passage of Shakespeare every Sunday at ten o'clock— you read one at the same time and we shall be as near each other as blind bodies can be in the same room.

John Keats (1795-1821)

There can be a kind of love, certainly devotion, between master and man. In Shakespeare's *King Lear* the courtier, the

Earl of Kent, in spite of being wrongfully banished by Lear, returns in disguise and continues to serve him.

Horns within—Enter Lear, Knights and Attendants

Lear: How now! What art thou? . . .

Kent: I do profess to be no less than I seem, to serve him truly that will put me in trust, to love him that is honest, to converse with him that is wise and says little, to fear judgment, to fight when I cannot choose, and to eat no fish.

Lear: What art thou?

Kent: A very honest-hearted fellow, and as poor as the King.

Lear: If thou be'st as poor for a subject as he's for a king, thou art poor enough. What wouldst thou?

Kent: Service.

Lear: Who wouldst thou serve?

Kent: You.

Lear: Dost thou know me, fellow?

Kent: No, sir; but you have that in your countenance which I would fain call master.

Lear: What's that?

Kent: Authority.

Lear: What services canst thou do?

Kent: I can keep honest counsel, ride, run, mar a curious tale in telling it, and deliver a plain message bluntly. That which ordinary men are fit for, I am qualified in; and the best of me is diligence.

Lear: How old art thou?

Kent: Not so young, sir, to love a woman for singing, nor so old to dote on her for anything: I have years on my back forty-eight.

Lear: Follow me; thou shalt serve me.

William Shakespeare (1564–1616):
'King Lear', I, iv, 9

Friendship has its funny side too: if there is any reader who has not yet read *The Diary of a Nobody* by George and Weedon Grossmith, then he or she is greatly to be envied. For my money, it is one of the funniest books in the English language. It recounts the daily doings of Charles Pooter who lives at 'The Laurels' in Holloway. The year is 1892.

April 27. Painted the bath red, and was delighted with the result. Sorry to say Carrie was not, in fact we had a few words about it. She said I ought to have consulted her, and she had never heard of such a thing as a bath being painted red. I replied: 'It's merely a matter of taste.'

Fortunately, further argument on the subject was stopped by a voice saying, 'May I come in?' It was only Cummings, who said, 'Your maid opened the door, and asked me to excuse her showing me in, as she was wringing out some socks.' I was delighted to see him, and suggested we should have a game of whist with a dummy, and by way of merriment said: '*You* can be the dummy'. Cummings (I thought rather ill-naturedly) replied: 'Funny as usual.' He said he couldn't stop, he only called to leave me the *Bicycle News*, as he had done with it.

Another ring at the bell; it was Gowing, who said he 'must apologize for coming so often, and that one of these days *we* must come round to *him*.' I said: 'A very extraordinary thing has struck me.' 'Something funny, as usual,' said Cummings. 'Yes,' I replied; 'I think even *you* will say so this time. It's concerning you both; for doesn't it seem odd that Gowing's always *coming* and Cummings always *going*?' Carrie, who had evidently quite forgotten about the bath, went into fits of laughter, and as for myself, I fairly doubled up in my chair, till it cracked beneath me. I think this was one of the best jokes I have ever made.

Then imagine my astonishment on perceiving both Cummings and Gowing perfectly silent, and without a smile on their faces. After rather an unpleasant pause, Cummings, who had opened a cigar-case, closed it up again and said: 'Yes—I think, after that, I *shall* be going, and I am sorry I fail to see the fun of your jokes.' Gowing said he didn't mind a joke when it wasn't rude, but a pun on a name, to his thinking, was certainly a little wanting in good taste. Cummings followed it up by saying, if it had been said by anyone else but myself, he shouldn't have entered the house again. This rather unpleasantly terminated what might have been a cheerful evening. However, it was as well they went, for the charwoman had finished up the remains of the cold pork.

George and Weedon Grossmith:
'The Diary of a Nobody'

An intimate glimpse of friendship from eighteenth-century country life. The gentle poet and letter-writer William Cowper living at Olney in Buckinghamshire writes to his dear friend Lady Hesketh:

My dear, I will not let you come until the end of May or beginning of June, because before that time my greenhouse will not be ready to receive us, and it is the only pleasant room belonging to us. When the plants go out, we go in. I line it with mats and spread the floor with maps; and there you shall sit with a bed of mignonette at your side, and a hedge of honeysuckles, roses, and jasmine; and I will make you a boquet of myrtle every day. Sooner than the time I mention the country will not be in complete beauty. And I will tell you what you shall find at your first entrance. Imprimis, as soon as you have entered the vestibule, if you cast a look on either side of you, you shall see on the right hand a box of my making. It is the box in which have been lodged all my hares, and in which lodges Puss at present; but he, poor fellow, is worn out with age, and promises to die before you can see him. On the right hand stands a cupboard, the work of the same Author. It was once a dove-cage, but I transformed it. . . .

I have made in the orchard the best winter-walk in all the parish sheltered from the east and from the north-east, and open to the sun, except at his rising, all the day. Then we will have Homer and

> Don Quixote; and then we will have saunter and
> chat and one laugh more before we die. . . .
>
> *William Cowper to Lady Hesketh*
> *9 February 1786 and 27 June 178*

A sidelight now on Samuel Johnson. When Mrs Thrale's
husband died she married Gabriel Piozzi, an Italian musician.
In 1786 she also published a series of lively pictures of her
good friend the Doctor.

Here she writes of his love of the poor.

> He [Dr Johnson] loved the poor as I never yet saw
> any one else do, with an earnest desire to make them
> happy.—What signifies, says someone, giving half-
> pence to common beggars? they only lay it out in
> gin and tobacco. 'And why should they be denied
> such sweeteners of their existence? (says Johnson).
> It is surely very savage to refuse them every possible
> avenue to pleasure, reckoned too coarse for our own
> acceptance. Life is a pill which none of us can bear
> to swallow without gilding; yet for the poor we
> delight in stripping it still barer, and are not
> ashamed to shew even visible displeasure, if ever the
> bitter taste is taken from their mouths.' In con-
> sequence of these principles he nursed whole nests
> of people in his house, where the lame, the blind, the
> sick, and the sorrowful found a sure retreat from all
> the evils whence his little income could secure them:
> and commonly spending the middle of the week at
> our house, he kept his numerous family in Fleet-
> street upon a settled allowance: but returned to
> them every Saturday, to give them three good
> dinners, and his company, before he came back to
> us on the Monday night—treating them with the
> same, or perhaps more ceremonious civility, than
> he would have done by as many people of fasion.
>
> *Hester Lynch Piozzi (1741–1821)*
> '*Anecdotes of the late Samuel Johnson*

There is a different kind of love and who better qualified than
Joseph Conrad to speak of it? Born of Polish parents in the

Ukraine, in 1884 he got his Board of Trade Master's Certificate
and became a British subject. He also mastered English prose.

The love that is given to ships is profoundly different
from the love men feel for every other work of their
hands—the love they bear to their houses, for
instance—because it is untainted by the pride of
possession. The pride of skill, the pride of responsi-
bility, the pride of endurance there may be, but
otherwise it is a disinterested sentiment. No seaman
ever cherished a ship, even if she belonged to him,
merely because of the profit she put in his pocket.
No one, I think, ever did; for a ship-owner, even of
the best, has always been outside the pale of that
sentiment embracing in a feeling of intimate, equal
fellowship the ship and the man, backing each other
against the implacable, if sometimes dissembled,
hostility of their world of waters. The sea—this
truth must be confessed—has no generosity. No
display of manly qualities—courage, hardihood,
endurance, faithfulness—has ever been known to
touch its irresponsible consciousness of power. The
ocean has the conscienceless temper of a savage
autocrat spoiled by much adulation. He cannot brook
the slightest appearance of defiance, and has remained the irreconcilable enemy of ships and men
ever since ships and men had the unheard of audacity
to go afloat together in the face of his frown. From
that day he has gone on swallowing up fleets and men
without his resentment being glutted by the number
of victims—by so many wrecked ships and wrecked
lives. To-day, as ever, he is ready to beguile and
betray, to smash and to drown the incorrigible
optimism of men who, backed by the fidelity of
ships, are trying to wrest from him the fortune of
their house, the dominion of their world, or only a
dole of food for their hunger. If not always in the
hot mood to smash, he is always stealthily ready for
a drowning. The most amazing wonder of the deep
is its unfathomable cruelty.

I felt its dread for the first time in mid-Atlantic
one day, many years ago, when we took off the crew

of a Danish brig homeward bound from the West Indies. A thin, silvery mist softened the calm and majestic splendour of light without shadows—seemed to render the sky less remote and the ocean less immense. It was one of the days, when the might of the sea appears indeed lovable, like the nature of a strong man in moments of quiet intimacy. At sunrise we had made out a black speck to the westward, apparently suspended high up in the void behind a stirring, shimmering veil of silvery blue gauze that seemed at times to stir and float in the breeze which fanned us slowly along. The peace of that enchanting forenoon was so profound, so untroubled, that it seemed that every word pronounced loudly on our deck would penetrate to the very heart of that infinite mystery born from the conjunction of water and sky. We did not raise our voices. 'A waterlogged derelict, I think, sir,' said the second officer, quietly, coming down from aloft with the binoculars in their case slung across his shoulders; and our captain, without a word, signed to the helmsman to steer for the black speck. Presently we made out a low, jagged stump sticking up forward—all that remained of her departed masts.

The captain was expatiating in a low conversational tone to the chief mate upon the danger of these derelicts, and upon his dread of coming upon them at night, when suddenly a man forward screamed out, 'There's people on board of her, sir! I see them!' in a most extraordinary voice—a voice never heard before in our ship; the amazing voice of a stranger. It gave the signal for a sudden tumult of shouts. The watch below ran up the forecastle head in a body, the cook dashed out of the galley. Everybody saw the poor fellows now. They were there! And all at once our ship, which had the well-earned name of being without a rival for speed in light winds, seemed to us to have lost power of motion, as if the sea, becoming vicious, had clung to her sides. And yet she moved. Immensity, the inseparable companion of a ship's life, chose that day to breathe upon her as gently as a sleeping child. The clamour of our excitement had died out, and our living ship, famous for never losing steerage way as long as there was air enough to float a feather, stole, without a ripple, silent and white as a ghost, towards her mutilated and wounded sister, come upon at the point of death in the sunlit haze of a calm day at sea.

Joseph Conrad (1857–1924): 'The Mirror of the Sea'

... Love will teach us all things: but we must learn how to win love; it is got with difficulty: it is a possession dearly bought with much labour and in a long time; for one must love not sometimes only, for a passing moment, but always. There is no man who doth not sometimes love: even the wicked can do that.

And let not men's sin dishearten thee: love a man even in his sin, for that love is a likeness of the divine love, and is the summit of love on earth. Love all God's creation, both the whole and every grain of sand. Love every leaf, every ray of light. Love the animals, love the plants, love each separate thing. If thou love each thing thou wilt perceive the mystery of God in all; and when once thou perceive this, thou wilt thenceforward grow every day to a fuller understanding of it: until thou come at last to love the whole world with a love that will then be all-embracing and universal.

Feodor Dostoevsky (1821–1881): from Father Zossima's discourse in 'The Brothers Karamazov'

To end this section on love and friendship Thomas Hardy in one of his jollier moods. I entirely agree with him about draught cider or cyder as he spells it. At the age of eighteen I was introduced at the Saracen's Head, near the great escarpment at Symonds Yat in the Wye Valley, to a brew known to the locals as 'stunn'em'. At threepence a pint it was nearly my undoing. On leaving the pub, I found myself teetering on the edge of a sheer drop and very nearly came to a precipitate end.

GREAT THINGS

Sweet cyder is a great thing,
  A great thing to me,

Spinning down to Weymouth town
　By Ridgway thirstily,
And maid and mistress summoning
　Who tend the hostelry:
O cyder is a great thing,
　A great thing to me!

The dance it is a great thing,
　A great thing to me,
With candles lit and partners fit
　For night-long revelry;
And going home when day-dawning
　Peeps pale upon the lea:
O dancing is a great thing,
　A great thing to me!

Love is, yea, a great thing,
　A great thing to me,
When, having drawn across the lawn
　In darkness silently,
A figure flits like one a-wing
　Out from the nearest tree:
O love is, yes, a great thing,
　A great thing to me!

Will these be always great things,
　Great things to me? . . .
Let it befall that One will call,
　'Soul, I have need of thee':
What then? Joy-jaunts, impassioned flings
　Love, and its ecstasy,
Will always have been great things,
　Great things to me!

Thomas Hardy (1840–1928)

SECTION FOUR

SECTION FOUR

COURAGE IN ADVERSITY

In the crucible of war.

COURAGE

O heart, hold thee secure,
In this blind hour of stress,
Live on, love on, endure,
Uncowed, though comfortless.

Life's still the wondrous thing
It seemed in bygone peace,
Though woe now jar the string
And all its music cease.

Even if thine own self have
No haven for defence;
Stand not the unshaken brave
To give thee confidence?

Worse than all worst 'twould be
If thou, who art thine all,
Shatter ev'n their reality
In thy poor fall.

Walter de la Mare (1873–1956)

An echo from the Civil War. Lovelace, a fervent Royalist
supporter, before setting out to battle, wrote these lines to his
fiancée Lucy Sacheverell. The message rings down the years:

TO LUCASTA, GOING TO THE WARS

Tell me not, sweet, I am unkind,
    That from the nunnery
Of thy chaste breast and quiet mind
    To war and arms I fly.

True, a new mistress now I chase,
    The first foe in the field;
And with a stronger faith embrace
    A sword, a horse, a shield.

Yet this inconstancy is such
    As you too shall adore;
I could not love thee, dear, so much,
    Loved I not honour more.

Richard Lovelace (1618–1657)

It might seem that 'Dad's Army' scripts owe quite a lot to
Shakespeare. Falstaff is conscripting villagers for the army.
Tough customers hold back. It takes Feeble, a woman's
tailor, to show them how:

Bullcalf: Good Master Corporate Bardolph, stand
    my friend, and here's four Harry ten shillings in
    French crowns for you. In very truth, sir, I had as

lief be hanged, sir, as go: and yet, for mine own
part, sir, I do not care; but rather, because I am
unwilling, and, for mine own part, have a desire
to stay with my friends: else, sir, I did not care,
for mine own part, so much.

Bardolph: Go to; stand aside.

Mouldy: And, good Master corporal captain, for my
old dame's sake, stand my friend: she has nobody
to do anything about her, when I am gone; and
she is old, and cannot help herself. You shall have
forty, sir.

Bardolph: Go to; stand aside.

Feeble: By my troth I care not; a man can die but
once; we owe God a death. I'll ne'er bear a base
mind: an't be my destiny, so; an't be not, so. No
man's too good to serve's prince; and let it go
which way it will, he that dies this year is quit for
the next.

William Shakespeare (1564–1616):
'Henry IV', Pt 2

To anyone who was ever a raw recruit in the ranks this is
where he came in:

NAMING OF PARTS

To-day we have naming of parts. Yesterday,
We had daily cleaning. And to-morrow morning,
We shall have what to do after firing. But to-day,
To-day we have naming of parts. Japonica
Glistens like coral in all of the neighbouring gardens,
 And to-day we have naming of parts.

This is the lower sling swivel. And this
Is the upper sling swivel, whose use you will see,
When you are given your slings. And this is the
 piling swivel,
Which in your case you have not got. The branches
Hold in the gardens their silent, eloquent gestures,
 Which in our case we have not got.

This is the safety-catch, which is always released
With an easy flick of the thumb. And please do not
  let me
See anyone using his finger. You can do it quite easy
If you have any strength in your thumb. The
  blossoms
Are fragile and motionless, never letting anyone see
        Any of them using their finger.

And this you can see is the bolt. The purpose of this
Is to open the breech, as you see. We can slide it
Rapidly backwards and forwards: we call this
Easing the spring. And rapidly backwards and for-
  wards
The early bees are assaulting and fumbling the
  flowers:
        They call it easing the Spring.

They call it easing the Spring: it is perfectly easy
If you have any strength in your thumb: like the bolt,
And the breech, and the cocking-piece, and the point
  of balance,
Which in our case we have not got; and the almond
  blossom
Silent in all of the gardens and the bees going back-
  wards and forwards
        For to-day we have naming of parts.
                    Henry Reed (1914–   ): '*Lessons of the War*'

The target comes into the gun-sights for 'the war to end war':

> ... When the troops arrived, singing 'It's a long,
> long way to Tipperary' at Maubeuge, after forced
> marches in the dark, it was one of the most
> tremendous moments I have ever experienced. *The
> most tremendous*. They swung up—or the tune swung
> them up—a very steep hill over the singing pave-
> ment, and the French came out and threw them
> flowers, fruit and cigarettes, and they looked so young,
> so elastic and so invincibly cheerful, so unmixedly
> English, so tired and so fresh. And the thought of
> these men swinging on into horror undreamt of—
> the whole German Army—came to me like the stab
> of a sword, and I had to go and hide in a shop for
> the people not to see the tears rolling down my
> cheeks. I couldn't let my mind dwell on it for days
> without the gulp in my throat coming back.
>
> I went to Mass this morning and it was nice to
> think I was listening to the same words said in the
> same way with the same gestures, that Henry V and
> his 'contemptible little army' heard before and after
> Agincourt, and I stood between a man in khaki and a
> French *Poilu* and history flashed past like a jewelled
> dream.
>
> *Letter from Maurice Baring to Dame Ethel Smyth:*
> *B.E.F., France.*
> *25 October 1914.*

Twenty-six years later, in the Summer of 1940, France fell in the Second World War. Britain stood alone. At least, the situation was clearer. King George VI wrote to one of his family: 'Personally, I feel happier now that we have no allies to be polite to and pamper.'

Of course, Churchill was now Prime Minister:

> What General Weygand called 'The Battle of France' is over. I expect the battle of Britain is about to begin. Upon this battle depends the survival of Christian civilization. Upon it depends our own British life and the long continuity of our institutions and our Empire. The whole fury and might of the enemy must very soon be turned upon us. Hitler knows that he will have to break us in this island or lose the war. If we can stand up to him all Europe may be free, and the life of the world may move forward into broad sunlit uplands, but if we fail then the whole world, including the United States, and all that we have known and cared for, will sink into the abyss of a new dark age, made more sinister, and perhaps more prolonged, by the lights of a perverted science. Let us therefore brace ourselves to our duty and so bear ourselves that if the British Commonwealth and Empire lasts for a thousand years men will still say: 'This was their finest hour.'
>
> *Winston Churchill to the House of Commons,*
> *18 June 1940*

Richard Hillary was one of the Few who made it their finest hour. His testimony was one of the most human documents to come out of the last war. Here, the young R.A.F. pilot experiences a blitz on London:

> There was a heavy air-raid on. . . . I turned and looked on a heap of bricks and mortar, wooden beams and doors, and one framed picture, unbroken. It was the first time that I had seen a building newly blasted. . . . We dug, or rather we pushed, pulled, heaved, and strained, I somewhat ineffectually

because of my hands; I don't know for how long, but I suppose for a short enough while. And yet it seemed endless. From time to time I was aware of figures round me: an A.R.P. warden, his face expressionless under a steel helmet; once a soldier swearing savagely in a quiet monotone; and the taxi-driver, his face pouring sweat.

And so we came to the woman. It was her feet that we saw first, and whereas before we had worked doggedly, now we worked with a sort of frenzy, like prospectors at the first glint of gold. She was not quite buried, and through the gap between two beams we could see that she was still alive. We got the child out first. It was passed back carefully and with an odd sort of reverence by the warden, but it was dead. She must have been holding it to her in the bed when the bomb came.

Finally we made a gap wide enough for the bed to be drawn out. The woman who lay there looked middle-aged. She lay on her back and her eyes were closed. Her face, through the dirt and streaked blood, was the face of a thousand working women; her body under the cotton nightdress was heavy. The nightdress was drawn up to her knees and one leg was twisted under her. There was no dignity about that figure.

Around me I heard voices. 'Where's the ambulance?' 'For Christ's sake don't move her!' 'Let her have some air!'

I was at the head of the bed, and looking down into that tired, blood-streaked, work-worn face I had a sense of complete unreality. I took the brandy flask from my hip pocket and held it to her lips. Most of it ran down her chin but a little flowed between those clenched teeth. She opened her eyes and reached out her arms instinctively for the child. Then she started to weep. Quite soundlessly, and with no sobbing, the tears were running down her cheeks when she lifted her eyes to mine.

'Thank you, sir,' she said, and took my hand in hers. And then, looking at me again, she said after a pause, 'I see they got you too.'

Very carefully I screwed the top on to the brandy

flask, unscrewed it once and screwed it on again, for
I had caught it on the wrong thread. I put the flask
into my hip pocket and did up the button. I pulled
across the buckle on my great coat and noticed that
I was dripping with sweat. I pulled the cap down over
my eyes and walked out into the street. . . . With
difficulty I kept my pace to a walk, forcing myself
not to run. For I wanted to run, to run anywhere
away from that scene. . . . I was drowning, helpless
in a rage that caught and twisted and hurled me on,
mouthing in a blind unthinking frenzy. I heard
myself cursing, the words pouring out, shrill,
meaningless. . . . Her death was unjust, a crime, an
outrage, a sin against mankind—weak inadequate
words which even as they passed through my mind
mocked me with their futility.

That that woman should so die was an enormity
so great that it was terrifying in its implications, in
its lifting of the veil on possibilities of thought so
far beyond the grasp of the human mind. It was not
just the German bombs, or the German Air Force,
or even the German mentality, but a feeling of the
very essence of anti-life that no words could convey.
This was what I had been cursing—in part, for I had
recognised in that moment what it was that Peter
and the others had instantly recognised as evil and
to be destroyed utterly. I saw now that it was not
crime; it was Evil itself—something of which until
then I had not even sensed the existence. And it was
in the end, at bottom, myself against which I had
raged, myself I had cursed. With awful clarity I saw
myself suddenly as I was. Great God, that I could
have been so arrogant!

Richard Hillary (1919-1943): 'The Last Enemy'

The Londoners were certainly indomitable. After one of the
biggest raids, Churchill toured some of the worst-hit areas.
On asking one old Cockney lady how she was getting on, she
replied:

'There's one thing about it, sir—these 'ere bombs
don't arf take your mind orf the war!'

This poem by Laurence Binyon captures marvellously the feel of 1942. A year later he himself was to die, aged seventy-four.

THE BURNING OF THE LEAVES
(1942)

Now is the time for the burning of the leaves.
They go to the fire; the nostril pricks with smoke
Wandering slowly into a weeping mist.
Brittle and blotched, ragged and rotten sheaves!
A flame seizes the smouldering ruin and bites
On stubborn stalks that crackle as they resist.

The last hollyhock's fallen tower is dust;
All the spices of June are a bitter reek,
All the extravagant riches spent and mean.
All burns! The reddest rose is a ghost;
Sparks whirl up, to expire in the mist: the wild
Fingers of fire are making corruption clean.

Now is the time for stripping the spirit bare,
Time for the burning of days ended and done,
Idle solace of things that have gone before:
Rootless hope and fruitless desire are there;
Let them go to the fire, with never a look behind.
The world that was ours is a world that is ours no
    more.

They will come again, the leaf and the flower, to
    arise
From squalor to rottenness into the old splendour,
And magical scents to a wondering memory bring;
The same glory, to shine upon different eyes.
Earth cares for her own ruins, naught for ours.
Nothing is certain, only the certain spring.

Laurence Binyon (1869–1943)

A long separation from loved ones is among the worst features of war. Alun Lewis, the Welsh poet who did not long survive, wrote this poem from his sick-bed in India.

IN HOSPITAL: POONA

Last night I did not fight for sleep
But lay awake from midnight while the world
Turned its slow features to the moving deep
Of darkness, till I knew that you were furled,

Beloved, in the same dark watch as I.
And sixty degrees of longitude beside
Vanished as though a swan in ecstasy
Had spanned the distance from your sleeping side.

And like to swan or moon the whole of Wales
Glided within the parish of my care:
I saw the green tide leap on Cardigan,
Your red yacht riding like a legend there,

And the great mountains, Dafydd and Llewelyn,
Plynlimmon, Cader Idris and Eryri
Threshing the darkness back from head and fin,
And also the small nameless mining valley

Whose slopes are scratched with streets and
   sprawling graves
Dark in the lap of firwoods and great boulders
Where you lay waiting, listening to the waves—
My hot hands touched your white despondent
   shoulders

—And then ten thousand miles of daylight grew
Between us, and I heard the wild daws crake
In India's starving throat; whereat I knew
That Time upon the heart can break
But love survives the venom of the snake.

                                   Alun Lewis (1915-1944)

Back some hundreds of years to be reminded by Sir John
Davies, a Wiltshire man, who was a poet of the school of
Spenser, and a Lord Chief Justice of the King's Bench, that
suffering can be a great teacher.

AFFLICTION

If aught can teach us aught, Affliction's looks,
　Making us look into ourselves so near,
Teach us to know ourselves beyond all books.
　Or all the learned schools that ever were.

This mistress lately plucked me by the ear,
　And many a golden lesson hath me taught;
Hath made my senses quick, and reason clear,
　Reformed my will, and rectified my thought.

So do the winds and thunders cleanse the air;
　So working seas settle and purge the wine;
So lopped and prunèd trees do flourish fair;
　So doth the fire the drossy gold refine.

Neither Minerva nor the learned Muse,
　Nor rules of art, nor precepts of the wise,
Could in my brain those beams of skill infuse,
　As but the glance of this dame's angry eyes.

She within lists my ranging mind hath brought,
　That now beyond myself I list not go;
Myself am centre of my circling thought,
　Only myself I study, learn and know.

I know my body's of so frail a kind
　As force without, fevers within can kill;
I know the heavenly nature of my mind,
　But 'tis corrupted both in wit and will;

I know my soul hath power to know all things,
　Yet is she blind and ignorant in all;
I know I am one of nature's little kings.
　Yet to the least and vilest things am thrall.

I know my life's a pain and but a span,
　I know my sense is mocked with everything;
And to conclude, I know myself a man,
　Which is a proud, and yet a wretched thing.

Sir John Davies (1569–1626)

IN HIS MENTAL ILLNESS, WILLIAM COWPER
FINDS HE IS NOT ALONE

I was a stricken deer, that left the herd
Long since; with many an arrow deep infixt
My panting side was charg'd, when I withdrew
To seek a tranquil death in distant shades.
There was I found by one who had himself
Been hurt by th'archers. In his side he bore,
And in his hands and feet, the cruel scars.
With gentle force soliciting the darts,
He drew them forth, and heal'd, and bade me live.
Since then, with few associates, in remote
And silent woods I wander, far from those
My former partners of the peopled scene;
With few associates, and not wishing more.

William Cowper (1731–1800): 'The Task'

George Wither raised a troop of horse for Parliament in the
Civil War. He was captain and commander of Farnham Castle
in 1642 and also wrote with sensitivity.

A WIDOW'S HYMN

How near me came the hand of Death,
　　When at my side he struck my dear,
And took away the precious breath
　　Which quickens my beloved peer!
　　　How helpless am I thereby made!
　　　By day how grieved, by night how sad!
And now my life's delight is gone,
　　—Alas! how am I left alone!

The voice which I did more esteem
　　Than music in her sweetest key,
Those eyes which unto me did seem
　　More comfortable than the day;
　　　Those now by me, as they have been,
　　　Shall never more be heard or seen;
But what I once enjoy'd in them
Shall seem hereafter as a dream.

Lord! keep me faithful to the trust
  Which my dear spouse reposed in me:
To him now dead preserve me just
  In all that should performed be!
    For though our being man and wife
    Extendeth only to this life,
Yet neither life nor death should end
The being of a faithful friend.

George Wither (1588–1667)

'n the other side a Royalist's wife writes a farewell letter to
·r husband who awaits execution.

My dear Heart,—My sad parting was so far from
making me forget you, that I scarce thought upon
myself since, but wholly upon you. Those dear embraces which I yet feel, and shall never lose, being the
faithful testimonies of an indulgent husband, have
charmed my soul to such a reverence of your
remembrance, that were it possible, I would, with
my own blood, cement your dead limbs to live again,
and (with reverence) think it no sin to rob Heaven
a little longer of a martyr. Oh! my dear, you must
now pardon my passion, this being my last (oh
fatal word!) that ever you will receive from me;
and know, that until the last minute that I can
imagine you shall live, I shall sacrifice the prayers
of a Christian, and the groans of an afflicted wife.
And when you are not (which sure by sympathy I
shall know), I shall wish my own dissolution with
you, so that we may go hand in hand to Heaven.
'Tis too late to tell you what I have, or rather have
not done for you; how being turned out of doors
because I came to beg for mercy; the Lord lay not
your blood to their charge.

I would fain discourse longer with you, but dare
not; passion begins to drown my reason, and will
rob me of my devoirs, which is all I have left to serve
you. Adieu, therefore, ten thousand times, my dearest
dear; and since I must never see you more, take this
prayer—May your faith be so strengthened that
your constancy may continue; and then I know

Heaven will receive you; whither grief and love will
in a short time (I hope) translate,

My dear,

Your sad, but constant wife, even to love your
ashes when dead,

Arundel Penruddock.

May the 3rd., 1655, eleven o'clock at night. Your
children beg your blessing and present their duties
to you.

(*Her husband, John Penruddock, a Royalist who joined t
insurrection of 1655, was taken at South Molton, and b
headed at Exeter.*)

That great Elizabethan Sir Walter Ralegh wrote these la
lines on the night before his execution at Westminster on 2
October, 1618. They were found in his Bible left in the Gat
House.

Even such is Time, that takes in trust
Our youth, our joys, our all we have,
And pays us but with earth and dust;
Who in the dark and silent grave,
When we have wandered all our ways,
Shuts up the story of our days;
But from this earth, this grave, this dust,
My God shall raise me up, I trust.

Sir Walter Ralegh (1552?–161

Now, the quiet courage and solicitude for his family shown b
William Penn. After being banished from Oxford and sent t
the Tower for his Quaker faith, he obtained a special gra
from King Charles II, sailed to America and in 1681 founde
the colony of Pennsylvania.

Worminghurst, 4th of the 6th Month, 16

My dear Wife and Children,

My love, which neither sea, nor land, nor death
can extinguish towards you, most endearedly visits
you with eternal embraces, and will abide with you

for ever. My dear wife, remember thou wast the love of my youth and the joy of my life, the most beloved, as well as most worthy of all my earthly comforts. God knows and thou knowest it, it was a match of Providence's own making. Now I am to leave thee, and that without knowing whether I shall ever see thee more in this life.

Take my counsel to thy bosom:—

Firstly. Let the fear of the Lord dwell in you richly.

Secondly. Be diligent in meetings and worship and business, and let meetings be kept once a day in the family, and, my dearest, divide thy time and be regular. In the morning, view the business of the house. Grieve not thyself with careless servants, they will disorder thee, rather pay them and let them go. It is best to avoid many words, which I know wound the soul.

Thirdly. Cast up thy income and see what it daily amounts to, and I beseech thee live low and sparingly until my debts are paid. I write not as doubtful of thee, but to quicken thee.

Fourthly. My dearest, let me recommend to thy care the dear children abundantly beloved of me. Breed them up in the love of virtue. I had rather they were homely than finely bred. Religion in the heart leads into true civility, teaching men and women to be mild and courteous.

Fifthly. Breed them up in love one of another. Tell them it is the charge I left behind me. Tell them it was my counsel, they should be tender and affectionate one to another. For their learning be liberal, spare no cost. Rather keep an ingenuous person in the house to teach them, than send them to schools, too many evil impressions being commonly received there. And now, dear children, be obedient to your dear mother, whose virtue and good name is an honour to you, for she hath been exceeded by none in integrity, industry and virtue, and good understanding, qualities not usual among women of her worldly condition and quality. Be temperate in all things, watch against anger, and avoid flatterers, who are thieves in disguise. Be plain in your apparel, let your virtue be your ornament.

Be not busy-bodies, meddle not with other folk's
manners, and for you who are likely to be con-
cerned in the Government of Pennsylvania, especiall
my first born, be lowly, diligent and tender. Keep
upon the square, for God sees you. Use no tricks,
but let your heart be upright before the Lord. So
may my God, who hath blessed me with abundant
mercies, guide you by His counsel, bless you, and
bring you to His eternal glory. So farewell to my
thrice beloved wife and children.

Yours as God pleaseth, which no waters can
quench, no time forget, nor distance wear away, but
remains for ever.

William Penn (1644-171

The lonely courage of a man who, for his faith, defies a
omnipotent state is perhaps the highest kind of all. Dietric
Bonhoeffer was a Christian martyr of the last war. A fier
critic of the Nazi regime, he was arrested in 1943 and hange
only a few days before his prison was liberated in 1945.

MORNING PRAYERS FOR FELLOW-
PRISONERS

CHRISTMAS 1943

O God, early in the morning I cry to you.
Help me to pray
And to concentrate my thoughts on you;
I cannot do this alone.

In me there is darkness,
But with you there is light;
I am lonely, but you do not leave me;
I am feeble in heart, but with you there is help;
I am restless, but with you there is peace.
In me there is bitterness, but with you there is
    patience;
I do not understand your ways,
But you know the way for me.

O heavenly Father,
I praise and thank you
For the peace of the night;
I praise and thank you for this new day;
I praise and thank you for all your goodness
and faithfulness throughout my life.

You have granted me many blessings;
Now let me also accept what is hard
from your hand.
You will lay on me no more
than I can bear.
You make all things work together for good
for your children.

Lord Jesus Christ,
You were poor
and in distress, a captive and forsaken as I am.
You know all man's troubles;
You abide with me
when all men fail me;
You remember and seek me;
It is your will that I should know you
and turn to you.
Lord, I hear your call and follow;
Help me.

O Holy Spirit,
Give me faith that will protect me
from despair, from passions, and from vice;
Give me such love for God and men
as will blot out all hatred and bitterness;
Give me the hope that will deliver me
from fear and faint-heartedness.

O holy and merciful God,
my Creator and Redeemer,
my Judge and Saviour,
You know me and all that I do.
You hate and punish evil without respect of persons
in this world and the next;
You forgive the sins of those
who sincerely pray for forgiveness;

You love goodness, and reward it on this earth
with a clear conscience,
and, in the world to come,
with a crown of righteousness.

I remember in your presence all my loved ones,
my fellow-prisoners, and all who in this house
perform their hard service;
Lord, have mercy.
Restore me to liberty,
and enable me so to live now
that I may answer before you and before men.
Lord, whatever this day may bring,
Your name be praised.
Amen.

Dietrich Bonhoeffer (1906–1945):
'Letters and Papers from Prison'

Alexander Solzhenitsyn is a man of much the same mettle as
Bonhoeffer. He too resisted an all-powerful state. After years
in Soviet prisons, and thanks largely to world opinion, he now
breathes again.

FREEDOM TO BREATHE

A shower fell in the night and now dark clouds drift
across the sky, occasionally sprinkling a fine film of
rain.

I stand under an apple-tree in blossom and I
breathe. Not only the apple-tree but the grass round it
glistens with moisture; words cannot describe the
sweet fragrance that pervades the air. Inhaling as
deeply as I can, the aroma invades my whole being;
I breathe with my eyes open, I breathe with my eyes
closed—I cannot say which gives me the greater
pleasure.

This, I believe, is the single most precious freedom
that prison takes away from us: the freedom to
breathe freely, as I now can. No food on earth, no
wine, not even a woman's kiss is sweeter to me than
this air steeped in the fragrance of flowers, of
moisture and freshness.

No matter that this is only a tiny garden, hemmed in by five-storey houses like cages in a zoo. I cease to hear the motorcycles backfiring, the radios whining, the burble of loudspeakers. As long as there is fresh air to breathe under an apple-tree after a shower, we may survive a little longer.

Alexander Solzhenitsyn (1918–):
'Stories and Prose Poems'

The nightmare of the fifty-three-year-old Dutch industrialist Dr Tiede Herrema began on 3 October, 1975 when his car was intercepted by gunmen as he drove to his factory on the outskirts of Limerick. After his eighteen-day ordeal as a hostage in the boxroom of a house at Monasterevin, Co. Kildare, during which his two besieged kidnappers threatened him with death several times, Dr Herrema still found it possible to say of them:

> I don't hate either of them. I see them as children with a lot of problems. I have children their age and if they were mine I would do my utmost to help them. I think that it is a pity they did this thing. Eddie Gallagher [one of the kidnappers] has to go to prison for a long time. That is a shame.

On 23 October, 1975, a bomb meant for somebody else exploded in a London residential street killing one of Britain's leading cancer experts, Professor Gordon Hamilton Fairley. His widow Daphne, mother of four, somehow had the courage to say:

> 'I feel no bitterness. We, as a family and friends, pray that his assassins and others may see the wastefulness of his and all other similar deaths, and that the rest of us in this wonderful world will learn something invaluable from our personal and terrible loss.' She then added these words: 'If you want to do something do it today. Say sorry, show somebody you love them now. If you had a row, make it up. Don't waste time—we didn't luckily.'

St Paul said:

> Blessed be God,
>   the Father of mercies,
>   and the God of all comfort,
>   who comforteth us in all our tribulations;
> that we may be able to comfort
>   those who are in any trouble,
>   with the comfort
>   wherewith we ourselves also are comforted of God.
>
> *2 Corinthians 1. 3, 4*

THE HARROWING OF HELL

'After sharp showers,' said Peace, 'how shining the
  sun!
There's no weather warmer, than after watery clouds.
Nor any love that has more delight, nor friendship
  fonder,
Than after war and woe, when Love and Peace are the
  masters.
Never was war in this world, nor wickedness so cruel,
But that Love, if he liked, could bring all to laughing,
And Peace, through patience, put stop to all perils.'

> *William Langland (1330?–1400?): 'Piers Plowman'*

SECTION FIVE

SECTION FIVE

NEW BEGINNINGS

This last section of the anthology speaks for itself.

> 'Why fear death? It is the most beautiful adventure in life.'
>
> *Charles Frohman: His last words before going down*
> *in the 'Lusitania' (7 March 1915)*

We are in 1903 and I am nearly seventy-one years old. I always thought I should love to grow old, and I find it is even more delightful than I thought. It is so delicious to be done with things, and to feel no need any longer to concern myself much about earthly affairs. I seem on the verge of a most delightful journey to a place of unknown joys and pleasures, and things here seem of so little importance compared to things there, that they have lost most of their interest for me.

I cannot describe the sort of done-with-the-world feeling I have. It is not that I feel as if I was going to die at all, but simply that the world seems to me nothing but a passage way to the real life beyond; and passage ways are very unimportant places. It is of very little account what sort of things they contain, or how they are furnished. One just hurries through them to get to the place beyond.

My wants seem to be gradually narrowing down, my personal wants, I mean, and I often think I could be quite content in the Poor-house! I do not know whether this is piety or old age, or a little of each mixed together, but honestly the world and our life in it does seem of too little account to be worth making the least fuss over, when one has such a magnificent prospect close at hand ahead of one; and I am tremendously content to let one activity after another go, and to await quietly and happily the opening of the door at the end of the passage way that will let me in to my real abiding place. So you may think of me as happy and contented, surrounded with unnumbered blessings, and delighted to be seventy-one years old.

Mrs Pearsall Smith: Letter from 'A Religious Rebe
Ed. Logan Pearsall Smi

Just as apples, when unripe, are torn from trees, but, when ripe and mellow, drop down, so it is violence that takes life from young men, ripeness from old. This ripeness is so delightful to me, that, as I approach nearer to death, I seem, as it were, to be sighting land, and to be coming to port at last after a long voyage.

Cicero (106–43 B.C.): 'De Senectu

... What if some little paine the passage have,
That makes fraile flesh to feare the bitter wave?
Is not short paine well borne, that brings long ease,

And layes the soule to sleepe in quiet grave?
Sleep after toyle, port after stormie seas,
Ease after warre, death after life does greatly please.

Edmund Spenser (c. 1552–1599):
'The Faerie Queene', bk.1, c.ix.xl.

DEATH, BE NOT PROUD

Death, be not proud, though some have callèd thee
Mighty and dreadful, for thou art not so:
For those whom thou think'st thou dost overthrow
Die not, poor Death; nor yet canst thou kill me.
From rest and sleep, which but thy pictures be,
Much pleasure, then from thee much more must
     flow;
And soonest our best men with thee do go—
Rest of their bones, and souls' delivery!
Thou art slave to fate, chance, kings, and desperate
     men,
And dost with poison, war, and sickness dwell;
And poppy or charms can make us sleep as well
And better than thy stroke. Why swell'st thou then?
One short sleep past, we wake eternally,
And death shall be no more: Death, thou shalt die!

John Donne (1571 or 72–1631)

LAST LINES

No coward soul is mine,
No trembler in the world's storm-troubled sphere:
I see Heaven's glories shine,
And faith shines equal, arming me from fear.

O God within my breast,
Almighty, ever-present Deity!
Life—that in me has rest,
As I—undying Life—have power in Thee!

Vain are the thousand creeds
That move men's hearts: unutterably vain;
Worthless as withered weeds,
Or idlest froth amid the boundless main,

To waken doubt in one
Holding so fast by Thine infinity;
So surely anchored on
The steadfast rock of immortality.

With wide-embracing love
Thy spirit animates eternal years,
Pervades and broods above,
Changes, sustains, dissolves, creates, and rears.

Though earth and man were gone,
And suns and universes ceased to be,
And Thou were left alone,
Every existence would exist in Thee.

There is not room for Death,
Nor atom that his might could render void:
Thou—THOU art Being and Breath,
And what THOU art may never be destroyed.

Emily Brontë (1818-1848)

The poplars are felled; farewell to the shade,
And the whispering sound of the cool colonnade!
The winds play no longer and sing in the leaves,
Nor Ouse on his bosom their image receives.

Twelve years have elapsed since I first took a view
Of my favourite field, and the bank where they grew;
And now in the grass behold they are laid,
And the tree is my seat that once lent me a shade!

The blackbird has fled to another retreat,
Where the hazels afford him a screen from the heat,
And the scene where his melody charmed me before
Resounds with his sweet flowing ditty no more.

My fugitive years are all hasting away,
And I must ere long lie as lowly as they,
With a turf on my breast, and a stone at my head,
Ere another such grove shall arise in its stead.

'Tis a sight to engage me, if anything can,
To muse on the perishing pleasures of man;
Though his life be a dream, his enjoyments, I see,
Have a being less durable even than he.

William Cowper (1731–1800)

AFTERWARDS

When the Present has latched its postern behind my
    tremulous stay,
    And the May month flaps its glad green leaves
        like wings,
Delicate-filmed as new-spun silk, will the neighbours
    say,
    'He was a man who used to notice such things'?

If it be in the dusk when, like an eyelid's soundless
    blink,
    The dewfall-hawk comes crossing the shades to
        alight
Upon the wind-warped upland thorn, a gazer may
    think,
    'To him this must have been a familiar sight.'

If I pass during some nocturnal blackness, mothy
    and warm,
    When the hedgehog travels furtively over the lawn,
One may say, 'He strove that such innocent creatures
    should come to no harm,
    But he could do little for them; and now he is
        gone.'

If, when hearing that I have been stilled at last, they
    stand at the door,
    Watching the full-starred heavens that winter sees,
Will this thought rise on those who will meet my
    face no more,
    'He was one who had an eye for such mysteries'?

And will any say when my bell of quittance is heard
    in the gloom,
    And a crossing breeze cuts a pause in its outrollings,

Till they rise again, as they were a new bell's boom,
  'He hears it not now, but used to notice such
    things'?

Thomas Hardy (1840-1928)

So just as a good mariner when he draws near to the
harbour lets down his sails, and enters it gently with
slight headway on; so we ought to let down the sails
of our worldly pursuits, and turn to God with all
our understanding and heart, so that we may come
to that haven with all composure and with all peace.
And our own nature gives us a good lesson in gentleness, in so far as there is in such a death no pain,
nor any bitterness; but as a ripe apple lightly and
without violence detaches itself from its bough, so
our soul severs itself without suffering from the
body where it has dwelt.

Dante (1265-1321)

THE DYING CHRISTIAN TO HIS SOUL

I

Vital spark of heav'nly flame!
Quit, oh quit this mortal frame:
Trembling, hoping, ling'ring, flying,
Oh the pain, the bliss of dying!
Cease, fond Nature, cease thy strife,
And let me languish into life.

II

Hark! they whisper; Angels say,
Sister Spirit, come away.
What is this absorbs me quite?
Steals my senses, shuts my sight,
Drowns my spirits, draws my breath?
Tell me, my Soul, can this be Death?

III

The world recedes; it disappears!
Heav'n opens on my eyes! my ears
  With sound seraphic ring:

Lend, lend your wings! I mount! I fly!
O Grave! where is thy Victory?
O Death! where is thy Sting?

Alexander Pope (1688-1744)

wo lifelong friends discuss their attitude to the meaning of
e in Tolstoy's *War and Peace*.

 ... Do you believe in a future life? he asked. In a
future life? repeated Prince André: but Pierre gave
him no time to answer, taking this repetition of his
own words for a negation all the more readily
because in earlier days he had known the Prince's
atheistical convictions.
 You say that you cannot see the kingdom of goodness and truth on earth. Neither have I seen it: nor
is it possible for any one to see it who looks upon
this life as the sum and end of all. On the earth,
that is to say on this earth (Pierre pointed to the
fields), there is no truth; all is falsehood and evil:
but in the universe, in the whole universe, truth has
its kingdom; and we who are now children of the
earth are none the less children of the universe. Do
not I feel in my soul that I am actually a member of
this vast harmonious whole? Do not I feel that in
this countless assemblage of beings, wherein the
Divinity, the First Cause—or however you may
term it—is manifested. I make one link, one step
between the lower beings and the higher? If I see,
and clearly see the ladder leading from plant to
man, then why must I suppose that it breaks off at
me, and does not lead on further and beyond? I feel
not only that I cannot utterly perish, since nothing
in the universe is annihilated, but that I always shall
be, and always was. I feel that besides me are spirits
that live above me, and that in this universe there is
truth.
 Yes, that is Herder's doctrine, said Prince André;
but it is not that, my friend, that will convince me,—
life and death—they are what convince a man. The
sort of thing that convinces a man is when he sees a
being dear to him, with whose life he has been

137

intimately bound up, to whom he has done a wrong, and has wished to make atonement (Prince André's voice trembled and he turned away), and suddenly this being suffers, is tortured and ceases to be.— Why? It cannot be that there is no answer. And I believe that there is one. That is what convinces a man. That is what has convinced me, said Prince André.

Why, certainly, that is it, said Pierre: is not that just what I was saying?

No. I only say that it is not arguments that convince one of the necessity of a future life, but the fact that one has been going thro' life in fond companionship with another, and suddenly that dear one vanishes, *there, into the nowhere*; and you yourself are left on the brink of the chasm looking down into it. And I have looked.

Well, and what then? You have known a *There* and a *Someone*. The *There* is the future life, the *Someone* God.

Prince André did not reply. The carriage and horse had long been led out on to the further bank, and were already harnessed, the sun was half-sunken beneath the horizon, and the evening frost was beginning to incrust the little pools on the shore with starry crystals, while Pierre and André, to the astonishment of the servants, coachmen and ferrymen, still stood in the boat talking.

If God and the future life exist, then truth and virtue exist; and man's highest happiness consists in striving for their attainment. One must live, said Pierre, one must love, one must believe that we live not merely now on this patch of earth, but that we have lived and shall live eternally there in the universe. He pointed to the sky.

Prince André stood leaning on the rail of the ferry-boat and listening to Pierre. He never moved his eyes, but gazed at the red reflection of the sun in the dark-blue flood. Pierre ceased speaking. All was silent. The ferry-boat lay drifted along the bank, and only the ripples of the current could be heard lapping feebly against its sides. Prince André fancied that this patter of the water babbled a

refrain to Pierre's words 'That is sooth, accept it:
that is sooth, accept it'.

Leo Tolstoy (1828–1910): 'War and Peace'

In this world (the *Isle of Dreames*)
While we sit by sorrowes streames,
Teares and terrors are our theames
                    Reciting:

But when once from hence we flie,
More and more approaching nigh
Unto young Eternitie
                    Uniting:

In that *whiter Island* where
Things are evermore sincere;
Candour here, and lustre there
                    Delighting: ...

There in calm and cooling sleep
We our eyes shall never steep;
But eternall watch shall keep,
                    Attending

Pleasures, such as shall pursue
Me immortaliz'd, and you;
And fresh joyes, as never too
                    Have ending.

Robert Herrick (1591–1674): 'The White Island'

ocrates, just before his execution, has been narrating a myth
oncerning the condition of souls in the next world, and this is
is comment on it:

> ... The moral of the whole story, Simmias, is this:
> that we should do all that we can to partake of
> Virtue and Wisdom in this life. Fair is the prize,
> and the hope great. Not that I insist upon all the
> particulars of my tale,—no sensible man would; but
> that it or something like it is true concerning our
> souls and their mansions after death,—since we are

agreed that the soul is immortal—this, it seems to me, is a proper opinion and enough to justify some venture of imagination in a believer. For the venture is noble: and it is right to relate such things, and fortify oneself as with enchantments. It was for this reason that I told the myth at so great length.

Wherefore a man should be of good cheer about his soul, if in this life he has despised all bodily pleasures and ornaments as alien to her, and to the perfecting of the life that he has chosen. He will have zealously applied himself to Understanding, and having adorned his soul not with any foreign ornament but with her own proper jewels, Temperance, Justice, Courage, Nobility and Truth, he awaits thus prepared his journey to Hades. . . . But a little while and you, Simmias and Cebes, and the rest of my friends will be departing: Me already, as they say on the stage, fate is calling: and in a few minutes I must go to the bath; for I think I had better bathe before drinking the poison, and not give the women the trouble of washing my body after I am dead.

Plato (427–348 B.C.): 'Phaedo

And here Plato himself faces death.

Wherefore, O judges, be of good cheer about death, and know of a certainty, that no evil can happen to a good man, either in life or after death. He and his are not neglected by the gods; nor has my own approaching end happened by mere chance. But I see clearly that the time had arrived when it was better for me to die and be released from trouble; wherefore the oracle gave no sign. For which reason, also, I am not angry with my condemners, or with my accusers; they have done me no harm, although they did not mean to do me any good; and for this I may gently blame them.

Still I have a favour to ask of them. When my sons are grown up, I would ask you, O my friends, to punish them; and I would have you trouble them, as I have troubled you, if they seem to care about riches, or anything, more than about virtue; or if they pretend to be something when they are really

nothing—then reprove them, as I have reproved you,
for not caring about that for which they ought to
care, and thinking that they are something when
they are really nothing. And if you do this, both I
and my sons will have received justice at your hands.

The hour of departure has arrived, and we go our
ways—I to die, and you to live. Which is better God
only knows.

Plato (427–348 B.C.): 'The Apology'.
Transl. by Benjamin Jowett

PEACE

My soul, there is a country
  Far beyond the stars,
Where stands a wingèd sentry
  All skilful in the wars:
There above noise and danger
  Sweet Peace sits crowned with smiles,
And One born in a manger
  Commands the beauteous files.
He is thy gracious friend
  And—O my soul, awake!—
Did in pure love descend
  To die here for thy sake.
If thou canst get but thither,
  There grows the flower of Peace,
The Rose that cannot wither,
  Thy fortress, and thy ease.
Leave then thy foolish ranges,
  For none can thee secure,
But one who never changes,
  Thy God, thy life, thy cure.

Henry Vaughan (1621–1695)

AND DEATH SHALL HAVE NO DOMINION

And death shall have no dominion.
Dead men naked they shall be one
With the man in the wind and the west moon;
When their bones are picked clean and the clean
  bones gone,
They shall have stars at elbow and foot;

Though they go mad they shall be sane,
Though they sink through the sea they shall rise
    again;
Though lovers be lost love shall not;
And death shall have no dominion.

And death shall have no dominion.
Under the windings of the sea
They lying long shall not die windily;
Twisting on racks when sinews give way,
Strapped to a wheel, yet they shall not break;
Faith in their hands shall snap in two,
And the unicorn evils run them through;
Split all ends up they shan't crack;
And death shall have no dominion.

And death shall have no dominion.
No more may gulls cry at their ears
Or waves break loud on the seashores;
Where blew a flower may a flower no more
Lift its head to the blows of the rain;
Though they be mad and dead as nails,
Heads of the characters hammer through daisies;
Break in the sun till the sun breaks down,
And death shall have no dominion.

Dylan Thomas (1914–1953)

FIDELE

Fear no more the heat o' the Sun,
Nor the furious Winter's rages;
Thou thy worldly task hast done,
Home art gone, and ta'en thy wages.
Golden Lads and Girls all must,
As Chimney-Sweepers, come to dust.

Fear no more the frown o' the Great,
Thou art past the Tyrant's stroke;
Care no more to clothe and eat;
To thee the Reed is as the Oak:
The Sceptre, Learning, Physicke must
All follow this, and come to dust.

Fear no more the Lightning flash,
Nor the all-dreaded Thunder-stone;
Fear not Slander, Censure rash,
Thou hast finish'd joy and moan.
All Lovers young, all Lovers must
Consign to thee, and come to dust. . . .

William Shakespeare (1564–1616)

ACKNOWLEDGEMENTS

Acknowledgement is gratefully made for permission to include the following works or extracts from them:

Payne, Robert: passage from *Schweitzer Hero of Africa* (Robert Hale Ltd and David Higham Assoc. Ltd).

Hyde, Lawrence: passage from *The Prospects of Humanism* (Mr Lawrence Hyde).

Causley, Charles: *Kings College Chapel* (by permission of Macmillan Co. and David Higham Assoc. Ltd).

Chardin, Pierre Teilhard de: Passage from *Le Milieu Divin* (Collins & Sons Co. Ltd).

Lawrence, D. H.: 'Pax' and 'Snake' from *The Complete Poems* (Laurence Pollinger Ltd and the Estate of the Late Mrs Frieda Lawrence).

Eliot, T. S.: 'Journey of the Magi' from *Collected Poems 1909–1962* (Faber & Faber Ltd).

King, Martin Luther: from an article printed in 'The Pacifist Conscience', Chicago, Ill., in April 1960 (*The Christian Century* and Ms. Joan Daves).

cummings, e. e.: 'i am a little church' from *Complete Poems 1913–1962* (MacGibbon & Kee and Granada Publishing Ltd).

MacDonell, A. G.: extract from *England, Their England* (Macmillan, London and Basingstoke).

Muggeridge, Malcolm: Mother Theresa's prayers from *Something Beautiful for God* (William Collins & Sons Ltd).

Brett Young, Francis: 'Atlantic Charter' from *The Island* (William Heinemann Ltd and David Higham Assoc. Ltd).

Bridges, Robert: extract from 'The Testament of Beauty' from *The Poetical Works of Robert Bridges* (Oxford University Press).

Moorman, J. R. H.: extract from *The New Fioretti* (Dr Moorman and the S.P.C.K.).

Cornford, Frances: 'Féri Bekassy' from *Collected Poems* (Barrie & Jenkins).

Harvey, F. W.: 'Ducks' from *Ducks and other Poems* (Sidgwick & Jackson Ltd).

Hardy, Thomas: passage from *The Return of the Native* and from *Far from the Madding Crowd* (The Trustees of the Hardy Estate and Macmillan, London and Basingstoke).

Sassoon, Siegfried: 'Man and Dog' from *Collected Poems 1908–1956* (G. T. Sassoon).

Munro, Harold: 'Milk for the Cat' from *Collected Poems* (Gerald Duckworth & Co. Ltd).

Davies, W. H.: 'On a Cold Day' from *The Complete Poems of W. H. Davies* (Jonathan Cape Ltd and Mrs H. M. Davies).

Thomas, R. S.: 'A Blackbird Singing' (Mr R. S. Thomas and Rupert Hart-Davis Ltd/Granada Publishing Ltd).

Morris, Ivan: Trans. and ed. of *The Pillow Book of Sei Shonagon* (Oxford University Press).

Williamson, Henry: extract from *The Lone Swallows* (A. M. Heath & Co. Ltd).

Bryant, Arthur: 'The Cornfield' from *The Lion and the Unicorn* (William Collins & Sons Ltd).

Baker, J. A.: extract from *The Peregrine* (William Collins & Sons Ltd).

Kierkegaard, Søren: passage from *Edifying Discourses* (Fontana Books Ltd).

Wells, H. G.: passage from *Ann Veronica* (J. M. Dent & Sons Ltd).

Graves, Robert: 'A Slice of Wedding Cake' from *Collected Poems 1965* (A. P. Watt & Son on behalf of Mr Robert Graves).

Firth, Peter: 'To My Wife' from *Prism* (Mr Peter Firth).

Lawrence, D. H.: passage from *Phoenix* (Laurence Pollinger Ltd and the Estate of the Late Mrs Frieda Lawrence).

Bridges, Robert: 'Tis forty years . . .' from *Shorter Poems* (Oxford University Press).

cummings, e. e.: 'the great advantage . . .' from *Complete Poems 1913–1962* (MacGibbon & Kee and Granada Publishing Ltd).

Tynan, Katherine: 'The Meeting' from *Poems* (The Society of Authors and Miss Pamela Hinkson).

Hardy, Thomas: 'Great Things', 'Afterwards' and 'The Darkling Thrush' (The Trustees of the Hardy Estate and Messrs Macmillan & Co.).

Colette: Enid McLeod's translation from *La Naissance du Jour* (M. Maurice Goudeket and Secker & Warburg Ltd).

de la Mare, Walter: 'Courage' from *The Complete Poems of Walter de la Mare 1969* (The Literary Trustees of Walter de la Mare and the Society of Authors as their representatives).

Reed, Henry: 'Naming of Parts' from *A Map of Verona* (Jonathan Cape Ltd).

Waring, Maurice: Letter to Dame Ethel Smyth (The Trustees of the Estate of Philip Wayre).

Churchill, Winston: extract from speech by Sir Winston Churchill as reported in Hansard (H.M.S.O.).

145

INDEX OF AUTHORS

Addison, Joseph, 11
Anonymous, 5, 16, 19, 22, 36, 90, 91, 116
Apocrypha, The, 18

Bacon, Francis, 47
Baker, J. A., 71
Baring, Maurice, 113
Beaumont, Francis, 12
Binyon, Laurence, 117
Blake, William, 3, 63, 80
Bonhoeffer, Dietrich, 124
Boswell, James, 11, 21
Bridges, Robert, 50, 91
Brontë, Emily, 97, 133
Brooks, Phillips, 30
Browning, Elizabeth Barrett, 87
Bryant, Arthur, 54
Bunyan, John, 20
Burns, Robert, 84
Byron, George Gordon, Lord, 85

Causley, Charles, 16
Chalmers, Thomas, 7
Churchill, Winston, 114
Cicero, 132
Clare, John, 45
Colette, 94
Conrad, Joseph, 103
Corbet, Richard, 95
Corinthians, The Second Epistle of Paul the Apostle to the, 128

Cornford, Frances, 68
Cowper, William, 23, 101, 120, 134
Cummings, e. e., 33, 92

Dante, 136
Davies, Sir John, 119
Davies, W. H., 58
De la Mare, Walter, 109
Dickens, Charles, 24, 42
Donne, John, 35, 133
Dostoevsky, Feodor, 105

Ehrmann, Max, 34
Eliot, T. S., 25
Emerson, Ralph Waldo, 31, 32
Firth, Peter, 87
Francis of Assisi, St, 62
Frohman, Charles, 131

Goldsmith, Oliver, 14
Graves, Robert, 83
Gray, Sir Alexander, 67
Grey of Fallodon, Viscount, 58
Grossmith, George and Weedon, 100

Hamerton, Philip Gilbert, 4
Hamilton Fairley, Daphne, 127
Hardy, Thomas, 49, 55, 60, 105, 135
Harvey, F. W., 64

Herbert, George, 77
Herrema, Dr Tiede, 127
Herrick, Robert, 139
Hillary, Richard, 114
Hopkins, Gerard Manley, 74
Hyde, Lawrence, 15

Isaiah, The Book of, 63

Jefferies, Richard, 41, 70
John, The Gospel according to St, 9
Jowett, Benjamin, 93

Keats, John, 17, 40, 57, 98
Kierkegaard, Søren, 78
King, Martin Luther, 27
Kingsley, Charles, 16

Langland, William, 128
Lawrence, D. H., 22, 51, 88
Lewis, Alun, 118
Lovelace, Richard, 110

MacDonell, A. G., 12
Matthew, The Gospel according to St, 8
Meredith, George, 46
Monro, Harold, 65
Moorman, John R. H., 62
Müller, Frederick Max, 80

Pasteur, Louis, 4
Payne, Robert, 10
Pearsall Smith, Mrs, 131
Penn, William, 122
Penruddock, Arundel, 121
Philippians, The Epistle of Paul the Apostle to the, 4
Piozzi, Hester Lynch, 102
Plato, 79, 139, 140
Pope, Alexander, 136

Ralegh, Sir Walter, 122
Reed, Henry, 111
Robinson, C. H., 23
Rossetti, Christina, 24

Sassoon, Siegfried, 69
Schweitzer, Albert, 9
Sei Shonagon, 50
Shakespeare, William, 16, 96, 99, 110, 142
Shelley, Percy Bysshe, 80
Sheridan, Richard Brinsley, 84
Sidney, Sir Philip, 81
Solzhenitsyn, Alexander, 126
Spenser, Edmund, 132
Stevenson, Robert Louis, 20

Teilhard de Chardin, Pierre, 17
Tennyson, Alfred, 42, 71
Theresa, Mother, 28
Thomas, Dylan, 141
Thomas, R. S., 48
Thompson, Francis, 73
Tolstoy, Count Leo, 9, 137
Turgenev, Ivan, 86
Tynan, Katharine, 95

Vaughan, Henry, 141

Walton, Izaak, 67
Wells, H. G., 82
Westwood, Thomas, 45
Whitman, Walt, 32, 39
Williamson, Henry, 53
Wither, George, 120
Wordsworth, William, 44

Young, Francis Brett, 29